THIS TIME, THIS PLACE

THIS TIME, THIS PLACE

by Michael Allen

THE BOBBS-MERRILL COMPANY, INC.

Indianapolis/New York

THE BOBBS-MERRILL COMPANY, INC.
A Subsidiary of Howard W. Sams & Co., Inc., Publishers
Indianapolis/ Kansas City/ New York

Library of Congress catalog card number: 74-123221

Manufactured in the United States of America

For Priscilla, John, Thomas, and Sarah

PREFACE

Twenty years ago my wife and I went to Paris. I had just graduated from college. She had finished two and a half years, and we had been married only a few months. We were going to Paris to be expatriates Partly I suppose because my mother and father had been expatriates themselves in their youth. Partly because the United States was on the edge of McCarthyism and a mindless and demonic anti-communism was growing. But mostly because I had been born in France. I wanted to know if I was French. I wanted to know what it meant to be me.

I am not sure what happened, but in Paris my wife and I found ourselves more and more confronted with our own American heritage. One day we went to the movies. They were showing a newsreel of Korea, and the audience of students clapped when Americans were shown dying. Much as

I hated that war, I could not clap at Americans dying—Americans who, I suddenly realized, were my brothers. I knew then that I was an American, a white Anglo-Saxon Protestant American, and I could not escape my identity. I could only fulfill it.

So we came home to face America, to face ourselves. I went to work for *Look* magazine; my wife finished college. But it was not enough. I wanted to search deeper, and I was very conscious of the Protestant part of my WASP identity. I knew my ancestors had helped build this country. They had carved out Kentucky, fought on both sides of the Civil War, traveled the Oregon trail, and grown with the West. I had lived once with my grandparents in Oregon. I loved them and I respected their Puritan Protestant Christianity. I wanted to know what they had really believed, who they were. I wanted to know who the ancestors of Western culture were, what our heritage really was, and therefore where we now were. For me that meant seminary and a thorough education in Christianity. So I left *Look,* and we moved to Cambridge, where I enrolled in the Episcopal Theological Seminary. When I was ordained we came back to New York, and in 1959 I came to St. Mark's in the Bowery on the Lower East Side.

This book, then, is about eleven years at St. Mark's, the richest and fullest years of my life, years in which I struggled to find myself and to know what it meant to be an American, a Christian, a man now in this time and in this place.

Michael Allen
New Haven, Connecticut
1970

THIS TIME, THIS PLACE

1

In a bleak and forbidding nowhere, two little children stand alone, cold, afraid and lost. Then the song begins. At first it is very far away and very soft, and then it grows nearer, grows louder. It is the most beautiful song the children have ever heard, this sound in the middle of nothing, in the middle of blackness, darkness, bleakness.

The song continues and suddenly stars appear. Out of the darkness light shines, and it begins to get warmer. The song builds, and the sun appears. It is light and now they can see the landscape, soft, undulating, and brown, just brown. Not a single living thing to be seen anywhere. Nothing to be seen but a great lion pacing back and forth in the distance, singing his song. Then the sound grows louder still, and as it does, the grass appears, and brown turns into green. Flowers and bushes and trees spring out of the ground at the command of the song. Then the animals spring forth as if out of a deep sleep. They move toward the lion, drawn by his music, until they all surround him. And the children know they have joined in the creation of a new world. This is what creation is about, a great song and then life.

I do not know of a lovelier way of talking about creation and life than this story from C. S. Lewis' *The Magician's Nephew*, one of seven volumes of his Chronicles of Narnia—a children's classic to join *Alice in Wonderland* and *Treasure Island*. Lewis has created a whole world of naiads and dryads, of unicorns and centaurs, of dwarfs and talking animals, a world no one can ever find. When it chooses, it will find you. The stories are for children with imagination and still full of wonder. They are also for adults who need to know what theology is really about, who in their jaded imaginations need new images, like a great lion calling forth creation with a song.

Maybe this image can replace tired and worn images, images we hardly remember, much less believe, and which we no longer find useful. Because each of us at one moment or another stands in a dark and fearful place alone and wondering if life and light will ever appear, if anything will ever happen. Waiting for a song to evoke light in the dark and to populate our world with warm and living creatures.

A girl stood in a doorway sobbing. Inside the hospital room, her father lay dying. She had said good-bye to him in the morning. They had laughed and joked at the breakfast table. She had gone to school—and the telephone call had come, summoning her to the hospital to stand alone in the darkness of her own sadness to watch her father die of a sudden stroke. It was a long time before the light shone for her again. She had to believe it would. Many people and much love called forth her life again. What if nobody had cared? What if no one had ever sung a song for her again?

Those older images we once knew spoke of the same experience. They spoke of the great void, a great blackness and darkness, a vast emptiness. And everywhere water and no dry land. "When God began to create the heavens and the earth . . ." Over the void the creator broods and gives it shape and purpose and meaning, pulling out of the dark nothingness, life.

The story as Genesis tells it is not about a distant day, a geologic age, when God created the world and everything in it, but of the moment, every moment, when God—because only the creator of life is worthy of being called "God"—creates life and meaning out of chaos and darkness.

The Hebrew, perhaps closer to his world, more aware of life in image and reality, knew how poised we all are on the edge of the void. At any moment we can plunge into the darkness, into the primeval chaos. At any moment now some madman can drop the bomb or shoot a president and plunge the world into chaos. As each of us can be plunged into chaos by sudden death, by hopeless rejection, by incurable hurts. The Hebrew knew that some force, something he called "God," is always pulling us back from chaos. So the story of creation is also a promise of life to be, yet to come, of ages ahead when men will still believe in life and creation, and the song will still be heard.

The Hebrew knew this was true because day follows night. And night is the time when God relaxes his grip, when he lets creation fall back into chaos, when the Lord rests from the labor of holding back chaos and creating life. Then come the things that go bump in the dark, the shadows of death and fear, and the nightmares that have always haunted men as they wait for light and day.

And at the last moment just before hope fades, the Lord wakes and rescues his world again from chaos, bringing up the sun and telling us to begin again the quest for existence, for purpose, for meaning in an ordered universe.

If this myth will not do, still, somehow a man needs to come to terms with life. He needs some way of living that makes sense, that begins with observable reality, that knows about chaos and darkness, knows about fear and loneliness and the great cold of the primeval void next to which we all live. But also knows about hope and life.

These curious people, the Hebrews, our ancestors in history and faith, seemed to know how to look at the world honestly and severely, and very, very clearly, yet hopefully. And they gave us the gift of a religion which at the heart is no device for escaping the world, for avoiding life, but a way to deal with it and accept it and love it.

What other choices have we? We could say that creation was once perfected and so remains. Men have believed this. They have likened the world and all creation to a great timepiece ticking on through history in immutable order.

But that is to defy experience. It is to wear blinders. It is to see corruption and confusion, to see the chaos which we all fear—and in this moment of history fear unusually—and not to perceive. It is to witness and then deny. To see riots, and police repression in the ghettos, to see bombings in cars on the highways, of buildings on quiet residential blocks. To see angry young people, and even angrier old, hanging on to their privileges and their profits at the risk of increasing tension and bitterness—and still say all is for the best in the best of all possible worlds.

Or we can look at the world as a fading and dying planet, a world growing steadily darker and lonelier and colder and shrinking deeper into chaos and disorder. We can see our air gradually getting heavier with soot and gas fumes and industrial pollution. We can see our lakes growing silent and dead as the fish die from waste pumped in by city and factory. We can see the refuse piling up behind every billboard and every fence and along the side of the highways and deep in the Atlantic off New York. We can see all this as evidence of death soon to come and we can sink into despair.

Then we deny hope, we deny our own humanity, and a whole other level of perception. We deny the creative moment, the touches of beauty and life that come to us all. We deny music and we deny the countryside in spring. We deny poetry and children dancing, and mystic revelation, and love between a man and a woman as they hold each other's bodies in deep embrace. And life hardly seems worth living at all.

Perhaps, then, we could argue for C. S. Lewis and his great lion, pacing back and forth in all his splendor, calling forth creation with a song. Or we could argue for the Hebrew God whose great spirit broods over the chaos, forming it, shaping it every moment, every day of our lives. These myths speak of a darkness around us, and a darkness within us that always threatens to envelop us. They speak of the unconscious, of the nightmares we dream at night—and see in the day—of the edge of the irrational close to which we all live.

They never deny the evil we see. But they affirm the rational, affirm the creative in man, the possibilities that are inbred in each of us, waiting to be called out. Because these myths apply not only to the creation at some mythical beginning, but to ongoing life every day.

At the center of the Hebrew experience was the Red Sea—the birth of freedom for Israel. A ragged body of men and women, of nonpeople, were called out of slavery, summoned out of Egypt and death, to march to the Promised Land. On one side of the Red Sea they knew they were slaves with no future and no past—only the death ahead in the waters or the death soon to be meted out by the Egyptian army. And on the other side, across the water, they were free. The army was dead, the water protected them from chase—and ahead the Promised Land.

This is also the story of Abraham, called out of Ur of the Chaldeans to go to a land he did not know to find a whole new meaning for himself and his family, to find a new life. And in that other place he discovered that he had never really been alive before, not until he came to the Promised Land.

Curiously enough this is an American myth, too, that we were slaves once, called out of the jails of Europe, the ghettos of Russia, the blighted potato fields of Ireland, out of persecution in England and deprivation in Scandinavia—called from every kind of slavery and hopelessness to the Promised Land. There we marred it by making our own slaves and risked then, as we risk now, falling back into death and chaos by polluting the Promised Land and destroying it.

I remember my Methodist grandmother in Oregon. When I was a child, she used to tell me bedtime stories, sometimes from the Bible, sometimes from her childhood. And I could never tell them apart. She would tell me a story about Abraham and Sarah, or Isaac and Jacob, and I could never tell if these were uncles and aunts or great-grandparents, or characters out of the Bible. My grandfather's name was Elijah, and his mother's name Sarah. Grandmother's name was Grace, and she had a sister named Hope. And she had grown up on a farm in the Willamette Valley that sounded no different from the home of Jacob and Rachel, of Abraham and Sarah. How could a six-year-old ever untangle all that?

But now I know that I was not alone in my confusion. I think my grandmother could never quite get it straight herself. She was so deeply involved in her Puritan Protestant mythology that she was living it out in her life, and had been doing so from childhood. And so had her parents, and those Biblical characters she mentioned in the family tree. She knew she had been rescued from slavery. Her grandparents had wandered in the desert on the way to the Promised Land. And they had found it in Oregon, a land truly flowing with milk and honey, far more so than the original Promised Land in Palestine.

She knew what this all meant and she thanked God every day for real and tangible blessings. She knew that her ancestors had passed the test of affliction, and it concerned her now to pass the test of prosperity, not to forget how she came into such a land, not to forget where her bread came from, and her milk, and honey, and fruit, and her family, and those blessings we might forget and take for granted. She was a very beautiful woman who to her dying day never unscrambled the confusion in her mind between the old Israel and the new. And I am glad she did not, and I wish I could not.

Her feelings, her experience are very deep in the American experience. Abraham Lincoln, standing in the very center of the American myth, saw us as the chosen people, the people called out by God to bring freedom to the world, to bring government of the people, by the people, and for the people to mankind. He saw the glorious hopes, the potential of America as a Promised Land. But he also recognized the reality. He saw us creating an Egypt out of Israel, nurturing our own slaves in the land of freedom, denying all our best hopes and dreams. So he called us the Almost Chosen People, almost chosen because we called men and women out of Africa not to freedom but slavery, because we denied our own myth and our own truth, and allowed a cancer to grow in our bodies, ready to consume us and destroy us. We allowed our nation to slip back into the chaos from which we all come and to which we all threaten to go in this moment when we still pay the price for slavery, when we still live with a racism we cannot admit, much less correct.

It is as if men carry their own chaos with them and impose their slaveries wherever they go. Nobody ever leaves chaos behind, and the process of creation is always taking place. Yet curiously enough those Americans who have learned the most from our myth are the black people and all the oppressed in the land. They may still be the last best hope of mankind, those men and women who believe the myth, who believe in a creator God who will set his people free, who will break the chains of bondage. And their God, long ago rejected by the rest of us, refuses to accept our chaos which we create and maintain. He refuses to allow men to be slaves. He does call men out to freedom and dignity. And wherever brave men respond in dignity and freedom, the testimony to his presence can be heard.

Perhaps we should be thankful that the slave believes what the master refuses to believe. Because now as a people we surely live in chaos, unsure, afraid, cold and not knowing whether we shall live or die or whether we shall be slaves or free. Here we are a nation afraid of freedom when we see it given to others, afraid that in giving others a share in freedom, we will lose it, as if there were not enough freedom to go around.

There was a moment when signs were pasted up all over New York saying, "This is Wallace Country," and men acted then as if they believed it and wished to affirm it. And so we do now. Cars speed by with signs saying, "America, Love It or Leave It," as if we could ever survive by exiling our malcontents, who in ages past were our saviors. And other cars proudly carry the banner "Honor America" without questioning what we shall honor and what we shall not. And in Chicago policemen riot, and a nation sees them doing so, but denies it, and frees the police but sentences the victims to jail. And judges act as if they were the law, rather than servants of it, and everywhere we act like a beaten army retreating in panic on the field of battle, leaving behind everything that once was precious, forgetting the fate of beaten armies and beaten people.

But there are people in our midst who believe that freedom is our heritage, who are willing to demand it and are not afraid. Perhaps they have heard another voice. Perhaps above the Agnews and the Mitchells and the Carswells, above all the doddering old congressmen who strangle our freedom and protect us from phantom enemies, they hear another voice— calling men and women out of slavery into life.

I would like to think that the song is being sung by a great lion forever pacing the earth, his song mingled with other songs, some singing of tyranny, some singing of greed, others beguiling us into false securities, but his always the sweetest and the clearest. A great lion with the gentleness of a lamb, loving his creation and battling against chaos and all its attendant demons.

I could never ask a man to hold a view of life that did not accept the realities that we see, that did not allow us to struggle with brutal and hard truth, that did not allow us to see slavery and tyranny when it is there. Nor could I deny hurt, sorrow, pain when it is there. The only hope I can affirm is the hope that reaches into man's slavery and sorrow and pulls him out to freedom and life. And that hope seems to me to involve a great lion singing and asking me to dance to his song.

2

One of the loveliest films of our time, I think, is *Elvira Madigan*, photographed in soft, almost pastel colors, with a Mozart concerto always in the background. It is the story of a Swedish count who leaves regiment, wife, children, everything he has and knows for a circus tightrope walker. They run off in the spring. They love in the summer, and in the fall they die. The idyll is over. The harsh reality comes upon them. He cannot work. Nor can she. They have nowhere to go—and no place to return to. So they end their lives in suicide.

The critics loved it. The crowds came and watched and wept at the beauty, the soft and golden beauty of a brutal film. Brutal because it explodes in suicide and death. Brutal because love and warmth and romance turn to darkness and bleakness and horror at the end. But the critics liked it. And all agreed that it spoke of beauty, and another great film contemporary with it, *Bonnie and Clyde,* spoke only of brutality. And perhaps here is a little parable of our world and of some strange notions about life.

Bonnie and Clyde tells of two lost, angry, brutal child-adults striking back at a world which they fear and hate. Both grow up in poverty and humiliation. Neither knows how to love, how to be close to any other human being. And Clyde is impotent, not only in spirit but in body, and his only manhood is a gun with which to kill and not create. They rob banks, spread terror, kill and destroy, and slowly learn to love each other. Somewhere in the wilderness and death of their lives, a spark of love grows, and one day Clyde can make love to Bonnie, and at last he is a man. But too late. They are both cut down by the law and the society they hate.

Two films of love and life, but two different points of view. *Elvira Madigan,* with all its beauty, its soft colors, its Mozart concerto, speaks of life fading away, of love dying, of all men's hopes turning to ashes. It is life colored by approaching death. Life with nothing but a succession of losses and sorrows and hurts. As indeed it can be, if there is nothing more to say. If nothing else ever happens. If no love ever grows.

But *Bonnie and Clyde* speaks of a brutal way of life, of death and bitterness and hurt and sorrow, out of which comes love, brief perhaps, but nonetheless hope of something more in human existence.

Perhaps this is closer to the truth, that deeper truth that questions the illusion that we are alive, that we have something to lose, something to be snatched away from us. Because the greater truth may be that we have very little, any of us, until something more is called out of us, until life makes its demand and we grow into manhood and life.

So we listen to the Spiro Agnews and the George Wallaces

who play to our fears, who tell us "they" will take away our homes and our jobs and threaten our lives, when who is to say we are alive? Who is to say anything of any importance will be lost, when we have yet to gain the only real treasure of a rich and full life?

For somewhere in the midst of our common experience is the rare moment of beauty, the great work of art, the creative genius who opens to us another whole understanding of life, who reveals new depths of existence. Or the miracles of the New Testament, the moments of healing, the moments of light. They may be life. They may be what we all are and can be, rather than the rare, the unusual. And life as we know it— the *Elvira Madigan* softness that really is death, that goes nowhere but to the grave—is the illusion.

Martin Luther, that great peasant who in his feel for the earth and the solid realities of life could soar like an eagle, ended a sermon once this way: "Man says, in the midst of life, we die. But God says, no, my child, in the midst of death you live." He said no to *Elvira Madigan*. He said no to all the illusions that we live and love only to see life snatched away. And he said yes to the hope that in the midst of that death we all know too well, the murder, the chicanery, the corruption, someone is calling out, evoking life.

A child idealizes his parents, and then one day sees their clay feet, and the world collapses for him as he faces the truth, and in a certain sense he dies. But life also begins when he recognizes the truth—and then the greater truth. That his parents are mean and ugly and broken and hurt, but lovely and beautiful too, struggling to find some other level, some other depth of existence. Then he can begin to accept himself, because he has begun to honor his father and his mother, to accept their humanity and therefore his own. Then his days can be long in the land which the Lord God gives him.

A man cannot really be alive until his illusions disappear.

If he does not know that men are cruel, that society is corrupt, that criminals control our cities, and something criminal in each of us controls us more than we dare fully admit, then he knows nothing about life. He does not know that we are all dead—waiting for the promise of life.

Life needs to be called out. Life itself is being created every moment out of death, out of the dark and lonely place where each of us lives.

But men can only speak this way if they know something more. It may be precisely the moment of life that makes possible the acceptance of death. The great Reformation cry of the total depravity of man comes not from the gloomy, morbid imagination, but from the vision of life. It is before the glory of what is possible and what is glimpsed that man may see life as totally depraved.

This is what Luther is talking about. It is because in some strange way he caught a vision of the glory of God, of the glory of all the infinite possibilities, that he could speak of life out of death and hope out of despair.

So the story of the wedding feast of Cana speaks of the good wine coming at the end, and not the beginning. The wedding feast has begun, the guests have lived and loved together—and the wine runs out. As *Elvira Madigan* comes to its disastrous end. As we all see everything precious slowly die. But Jesus turns water into wine—and better wine, glorious wine, so the party not only continues, but grows richer and fuller. And this strange and seemingly innocuous story may be at the heart of the New Testament. For one commentator at least suggests that of the seven signs which dominate the gospel of St. John, this alone is followed by no explanation; the whole gospel provides its explanation. And the explanation is that life triumphs over death.

The healing stories of the New Testament are not exciting

because they are about healing as such. I have never understood the whole healing ministry in the church. I do not understand healing services, or why people want to be healed
in the narrow physical sense. Because the great excitement
is the healing which means new life. Jesus does not open
men's eyes alone. He gives men something to see, a new
world, a new hope, himself. He does not give men hearing
without giving them something to hear, his voice and his
truth. He does not give men their legs, except to call them to
walk with him. But what good is it to give a man his sight and
offer him only a ghetto to see, or his ears only to hear trite
conversation and petty lies? Or what good is it to give a man
his legs only to walk to the employment office and find again
that no job exists for him?

The New Testament is about a man who went to the dead,
who walked among them—the dead who have yet to be
buried, who hang around street corners with no hope, who
shoot up with heroin, who sit in dismal schools learning nothing, who sit glued to a TV that sells them products nobody
needs—and he gave them life. He confronted men who had
nothing to do and nowhere to go and made disciples out
of them, and they changed the content and the form of
Mediterranean society. In the midst of their death, they found
life. Like Genesis with its picture of the creator God bringing
form and life out of chaos and nothingness, the New Testament presents the man who pulls life out of the death of his
people.

So look at our moment. Will our politics go on being dominated by fear, fear of the Reds, of the blacks, of the hippies,
of youth, the fear of losing what we really do not have, life,
rather than the hope of gaining something we all desperately
desire, freedom and hope, and meaning?

It is exciting, then, and hopeful when black people, or any

people, wake up and demand life and walk in hope. Because
in their very walking they proclaim the possibility of the life
they demand.

I remember a Monday night in the midst of all the tensions
over New York's schools. The teachers were on strike. Parents
were pushing past teachers who refused to teach and open-
ing their schools and demanding an education for their children. All the apathy that crushed the school system of New
York was gone, at least for a moment. And thousands of us,
black and white, were demonstrating in front of City Hall. We
were demanding that communities in the city control their
schools, as communities in the suburbs control theirs. We
were demanding that all the differences among the children
of the city be recognized and dealt with creatively.

We walked across the Brooklyn Bridge, thousands of people headed toward the Board of Education offices in Brooklyn.
We laughed and we talked, and sometimes we almost danced.
Because we all felt the freedom and the joy of believing in
life.

We got there, and the speeches began, the rhetoric of
freedom—but greater still the action of freedom, because a
thousand people suddenly moved and started to walk. They
were heading for Ocean Hill–Brownsville, that embattled little
neighborhood which had held out for months for the right to
educate black and Puerto Rican children in their own pride
and with their own teachers and their own methods. But we
had miles to walk, and walk it we did. Every step getting
lighter, not heavier. Black teenagers swaggering and cavort-
ing because for that moment their lives meant something.
And I felt proud, proud to be part of a moment of life which
cast rays of light on all other moments of life.

It is beautiful when men and women demand an education
for their children. Lo, these many years in every ghetto of this

city or any other city nobody demanded anything at all. Good teachers and good principals among the many who were no good at all tried to drag parents into their schools, and failed. And now, black and Puerto Rican people were literally breaking down the doors of the strike-closed schools and demanding an education.

It is difficult for some of us to take. It requires enormous understanding and intelligence and restraint from those in power to allow life to happen, to allow life to emerge from death, and not to fear it, not to see it as evil or threatening. But to see the urgings of life in the midst of death.

C. S. Lewis is so close to the truth when he speaks of a world that is dark and forbidding and cold until it is created, until life stirs within it and men walk and then dance to the great song of creation.

It would be good if we could live and not be afraid of other men's freedom but delight in it because it speaks of our own freedom and our possibilities. But all this certainly challenges our understanding of life, of God, of creation. Because if God is indeed the God of creation, then all the stirrings, all the moments of life, are his moments, his creation, to be blocked at our common peril.

Perhaps the great film of my time, the one which moved me more deeply than any other, and the most profoundly Christian film I know is Godard's first, *Breathless,* the film that began the New Wave, and perhaps established what is now contemporary film. *Breathless—A Bout du Souffle—*is about breath, literally the end of breath, the end of life—where life begins. It is about that great Christian pun which is the word for breath, air, wind, Spirit, and therefore life. In both Greek and Hebrew one word stands for all these meanings. So the Holy Spirit is the holy breath, the holy wind—the life-giving breath of God.

The film is about a young hoodlum who fancies himself a Humphrey Bogart character, who steals cars and plays games with life. He steals a car in Marseille and heads for Paris, thundering down the road like a child with a new toy. And as he goes, he finds a revolver, a real one, in the glove compartment and he plays with it as a toy. He holds it up and points it at passing cars and says, "Bang, bang." Until the police start chasing him, and corner him. Then the pistol is real and he really pulls the trigger and a cop is really dead. And therefore the hoodlum is dead, too. For surely the cop killer will always lose his life in this and every other society we know.

Now he is condemned to death and he knows it. Death is no longer abstract or distant—and at the end of the film he dies from a police bullet. But before he dies, three days in Paris. Three days frolicking through Paris with an American college girl, living life fully and joyfully and triumphantly in the face of death.

But the girl is searching for the ultimate meaning of life and never finding it because she will not experience life and because she does not know she is dead. And she cannot really accept her young man with his gift of life.

There is a lovely scene of the two of them in bed. The hoodlum with his hat on and a cigarette in his mouth—and nothing else. And the girl telling him about Camus. "Who's that," he says, "your last lover?" And the poor girl does not know that life is not to be discussed and dissected, but lived.

So she searches for meaning and truth and interviews a silly novelist for a newspaper and continues the quest and denies the life the hoodlum offers her. And when he offers more than she can take, she turns him in and he dies before her eyes— for her.

On a table is a book, and the camera zooms in on it. The title of the book is: *We Are All on Leave from Death*. And perhaps the point of the movie is that the only certain fact we know is death. Every one of us will die. So we are dead. The only freedom then open to us is to live, to live in the face of death, to rejoice and to make new life.

And this I know: the stuff of life, the real basic decisions of life, the questions of ethics and morality and truth and beauty, are for the living and not for the dead. The great sadness of the American church is its attempt to preach life to the dead who do not want to hear of life, or live it. They will make no moral decisions. They cannot.

The film *Breathless* is about a wicked man, a hoodlum, but fully alive, and therefore ready to make the moral decision. Free to make it because he can choose. He can choose evil. He can choose good. And he chooses to die for his girl, die before her eyes.

We showed the film one night as part of our church's Lenten program. It was the beginning of new life at St. Mark's. We lost one vestryman that night. He got up in the middle of the film—I think when the hoodlum and his girl were in bed together—and walked out and never came back. But we gained the lives of some of our young. A lovely black teenage girl said wistfully when the film was over, "I believe that young man died to bring the girl out of a world of illusions into reality." And perhaps that is what the film was about, and certainly that is what the Christ story is about, bringing men out of the world of illusion into reality.

It is the living who know they are dead, who know that their life is by gift and gift alone, who make the decisions that can be deemed moral—or immoral. And for the dead there is nothing but to bury the dead. Because the creator God has given us this choice: in the midst of death man may live. This is what Martin Luther was talking about. This is what the great lion is singing about—a great song that evokes life and that calls us into being every day, that calls order and form out of chaos, and life and beauty out of death and ugliness.

To me this is the guts of the Christian faith and this is something to get excited about. It does not matter very much whether you call the creator God, or call him a great lion, or call him nothing at all. It only matters that you listen and respond. The result is that there are many men in this world who worship their Lord far better than Christians, and never know it. But they live.

In another of C. S. Lewis' books in the Narnia series, *The Last Battle,* the forces of good and evil are drawn up in battle, the last battle, the one that leads to judgment. And as each warrior dies, he meets his God. A warrior of the forces of evil whose God is the demon God Tash dies, and he meets not Tash at all but the great lion. He is startled and amazed, and the lion says to him, "You never worshiped Tash, my son. You never obeyed him. You were mine from the beginning and so you will be always."

Perhaps Lewis is thinking of the great parable of those who have given drink to the thirsty and bread to the hungry, who have visited the prisoners. The name does not matter much. Life is offered to those who wish to receive it. If they take it in God's name, then at least they know where they got it, and maybe can help others find it. But if they do not take it in God's name, at least they live—and many a man who knows God's name has yet to accept his life.

This is at the heart of the faith as far as I am concerned and the rest has to do with how you work it out, what it really means to be dead or alive. That's what ethics is about; that is what the whole rest of Christian doctrine is about; that is what worship means. I think liturgy is the moment in which we symbolize the call from death into life. That is what we mean by celebration. We celebrate the gift of life and the hope that it will last forever.

Paul Tillich in an article he once wrote for the *Partisan Review* said there are two kinds of religious men in this world. There are the negative religious, men of ultimate concern about life, about men, about the creation, those who ultimately care what it means to be human. And caring ultimately, they find the truth, and the truth leads them to despair. Because the truth is despair. It is death. But there are the positive religious, those who take the leap of faith and hear the call and live and hope, though all the evidence points the other way.

Negative religion is the minimal demand, the demand of honesty. And I do not see how a man can be fully human unless he is honest about himself, about his world, unless he sees the cruelty that all men practice, that he himself practices, unless he sees the pain and sorrow and suffering of his fellowmen. And if he does see all this, then the illusion of life must disappear. The illusion that we are alive, that someone will deprive me of my life and my property if I do not protect it, and that we will each die kicking and screaming had best be out of the way if a man will be human. Rather recognize that we live in a dead world. And then listen for the call to life. Listen for a great lion singing.

3

We stood in front of PS 63 on the Lower East Side watching the pickets scream and jeer. They were teachers on strike, trying to keep the school closed and the children out. They were blocking the sidewalk and the front entrance and nobody wanted very much to shove his way through. The principal was on strike, too, and they had the school shut down tight.

But the parents wanted the school open, and the law was supposed to be on their side. So they had found a teacher who was willing to be acting principal, and my job was to escort her in through the line of teachers and open the school. This was a very new experience for me. I had never crossed a picket line before. Certainly I had been on many. It is hard to avoid them on the Lower East Side, where we almost tell time by demonstrations and picket lines.

The teacher found it very painful to cross that line, and so did I. But somehow all the roles were reversed that day. So we went in. As we did, the pickets began to scream. They said to her, "How could you, Donna, how could you?" As if she had committed a mortal sin. And to some extent in her own eyes she had, because I could see something curl up and die inside her. I wonder about her now, whether she found life that day or not. And then an enraged teacher pushed her face close to mine and shouted, "What price your soul, Reverend?"

The confrontation was really wicked and soul-wrenching. The cops would not help. There was a sergeant standing by looking off into space and when I asked him to unblock the sidewalk and restore order, he said, "I don't see anything wrong." Maybe he found it as hard to face as I did.

Up at PS 40, which is above 14th Street and no longer the Lower East Side but a solid middle-class part of New York, Stuyvesant Town and decent housing, the parents were all being radicalized. It is one of the best schools in the city, very white, very middle class. The parents were law-abiding people who had always done everything by the book and they had been trying to open the schools that way for the last couple of weeks. But the school authorities were better at legalism than they. So the school had been closed since the beginning of the strike. Now respectable middle-class parents were breaking in the doors of the school and protecting their strike-breaking teachers as they went in.

The night before, one of the vestrymen of St. Mark's, a fine, austere gentleman who looks a little like a Scot's Guard officer, sat up in Wagner Junior High School, where his daughter went. He was protecting the school from the custodian and trying to be sure the parents could open it again in the morning. Another father, with his two teenage sons, was in there with him—and then the custodian sneaked in and took the fuses out of the main fuse box. They chased him all over the school and finally brought him down with a flying tackle and called the police, these two respectable guardians of their children's school.

But my bad morning was spent in the district superintendent's office. I was there with parents and teachers from PS 63, petitioning him to open the school—and obey the directives of the Board of Education. He had refused the day before and verbally beaten the proposed acting principal into the ground I had spent that afternoon trying to calm her hysterics. But I could not convince her to go back and try again.

Now we had another teacher who seemed prepared to take the district superintendent on. But she was very frightened, and the superintendent charged at her like a wounded bull. He was brutal and crushing and the teacher wavered. Another priest and I defended her and fended off some of the verbal blows, and we finally extracted consent from him to open the school in obedience to the Board of Education's instructions.

It was a very curious episode, and instructive about our manner of life. If we had taken a transcript of that meeting, I think the district superintendent would have come off very well—and some of us rather badly. His words were good. They were the kind of words gentlemen use, the kind we use in front of children. The rest of us, I fear, used some profanity and perhaps even obscenity. But if instead of a transcript, we were to use a tape recorder and blur the words and listen to the feelings, it would seem strange that we lived through the meeting. He should have been shooting at us. Because his emotional tone was savage and brutal and bestial, but unrecognized, as so much of our life is, clothed in polite words and verbal decorum—the emotion denied and refused. It is as if we did not know how to handle our feelings and wanted to bury them.

Perhaps this is what our young are telling us. They are saying that we have too long denied emotion and passion. A psychiatrist I know calls us, those of us who are over thirty, the "affectless generation," the generation that exhibits no overt feeling, no passion. Words, yes, lots of words, more words than most of us can handle. Confusing words, deceptive words. But no feeling.

Protestants know all about this. We are the most verbal of people. We have interpreted the Word of God as words, endless words—and no feeling. Hence the coldness and bleakness of so much Protestant worship, and the turning away of young people who yearn for something else, for some release from the wall of emotional silence.

A whole generation is reacting against parents who had no feeling or showed none, a generation that watched some of the great events of our time and showed no visible feeling about them, that looked at slums but did not see them. We knew about the war in Vietnam, but did not abhor the death that covers the nation like a shroud. And as our children and even some of our adults shout out their hatred of the war, the President of the United States, the symbol of the older generation, watches football on TV—the great spectator—while others live and die their precious lives.

I walked with thousands of young Americans toward the White House. We were protesting the American invasion of Cambodia. Here was the flower of American youth—the prettiest girls, the handsomest young men. And they were all singing softly, gently, "All we are saying is, Give peace a chance." It was a haunting and lovely moment, speaking of tender hopes, wide-eyed visions, deep yearning. And over against that, the hard-eyed cynicism of the President of the United States, hiding behind the rows of buses forming a protective ring around the White House. And our cynicism, those of us who tell our young that the economy requires war, that death is inevitable, that our youth must die to preserve the American way of life. And we try to make them as unfeeling as are we who mouth these horrors.

When young people smoke pot or trip on LSD, they are delving into an area we told them little about—expanding consciousness, expanding emotion. To smoke pot for many a young person is to find out that you have been playing Bach on a ten-key piano and now you discover eighty-eight keys and a new world of beauty. It might be soberly considered that mind- and consciousness-expanding drugs do just that—open up new worlds of feeling. And to that extent may be beneficial.

We might all be more capable of dealing with our society if we knew what we felt, if we knew the depths of our own experience, and the experience of others. A meeting with the district superintendent might have been less of a nightmare if we were more attuned to what we felt, more able to see what people really do to each other. And our young might be less angry if we honored their deepest feelings.

Young people I know are searching out their experience both inner and outer because something in them makes them doubt whether there is any experience at all. One of the great tragedies of the human race is that generation after generation we really do believe what our parents tell us. We who are parents never quite understand this, so we are shocked when our kids mirror back to us what we have said and lived. It is frightening to have our children tell us there is nothing to believe in, nothing to experience. And then use these strange drugs which open up life and feeling.

But what then? The drugs have opened them up. They tell us of new worlds, but what do we do in this new world we have discovered, how do we handle a whole new freedom for which we were not prepared? Now that we feel, can we act?

It is as if we were all being broken out of our security and out of our dullness and called to new life. We are surrounded by kids with long hair and funny clothes. Kids who walk by as if dressed for the Spanish American War or an Edwardian ball. Even policemen growing mustaches and beards and coming to their demonstrations in loud sport shirts and bizarre trousers in order to pass. And a whole segment of society has taken to the streets—mouthing obscenities none of us ever admitted quite existed, shouting and screaming. It is as if the unconscious were bursting out and the thin veneer that has kept us thinking that all is well—there are no troubles—were being shattered. We are being forced to face what our whole generation avoided and denied.

A hippie friend of mine sat in my office one day and explained to me that you have to smoke pot to live in New York, and I thought that was a rather grand generalization. But he went on to say, "Well, if you don't smoke, you can't connect with yourself. You sit in a chair in your room," he said, "and all you hear are the noises outside. The traffic, the people coming up the stairs. You hear all this terrible stuff and you can't make contact with yourself. But wow, get some good Vietnam grass . . ."

Think about that. Some of the best marijuana around comes from Vietnam. Is that what we went there to do?

So if you sit in a chair and smoke Vietnam grass, you can forget all the noises and the misery and the horror and be high on yourself and really live. He went on to tell me how much better it was to turn in on yourself and find yourself and live than to go out and venture into the hostile world. I asked him if he really wanted to leave the world in the hands of those people who go out and run it now, and he replied that it did not matter very much because he had only sixty or so years to live in this world and then . . .

The boy was stealing all the church's bad lines. And I, the Christian priest, had to deny the hereafter and try to tell him to live now and not some other time, not in some by-and-by world. But at the same time I wondered if I had any right to say that to him, because my generation had never told him he could fight for any great cause, or believe any great faith, or move out and do anything that really mattered. And every day we go on slapping down our young—as we destroy them in our war.

Another young man I know said to me one day, "You keep telling me it is foolish to fight with the school about the length of my hair. You keep telling me I should fight for serious causes. Like what?" And I wondered what any of us have told our children about the possibility of fighting for something more than haircuts.

We are all confronted with a new world we barely understand, a world exploding around us. New ideas and information hit us faster than we can possibly assimilate them. New people are born faster than we know how to feed them. And everywhere men are demanding freedom, the freedom from age-old patterns of life, of repression, of restraint. And it is too much for all of us, more than we can handle, more than we want to handle. But handle it we must. Because the change is upon us and it grows and demands more and more from us every day. What we could ignore yesterday, we shall not be able to ignore or escape tomorrow.

So now we are free, free to react to the world, free to challenge it, but afraid of our freedom, paralyzed by what we see.

As Lord Jim was paralyzed, Jim, the hero of Conrad's great novel of the sea and the innermost being of man. He was free, free to go to sea, free to challenge the world, free to shake off the old restraints, to know that life was larger than anyone ever imagined. And he was ready to dare it.

Jim was the first mate of an old rust bucket, the *Patna,* a ship with European officers and native crew, sailing the Indian Ocean, carrying pilgrims to Mecca. It was a beautiful night. The sea was calm, the passage uneventful, and Jim stood watch on the bridge. Then suddenly a crash, and the *Patna* came to a halt. She had hit something in the water.

Jim raced below to discover an old rusty bulkhead pulsating under the pressure of water. The bow was crushed in, the water coming in fast, and the old bulkhead too weak to hold it back. He thought of repairing it. But the rust was so thick and the metal so scaly that a beam laid against it might as much puncture it as protect it. That risk he could not take. And there was nothing else to do.

Back on deck, Jim surveyed the situation. He could not fix the ship and at any moment it would sink. In his imaginings he could see the pilgrims asleep, unaware of their fate. If he blew the alarm, they would wake and rush for the lifeboats, but there were not enough. Panic would inevitably follow. And he could see men and women clawing each other to death for space in a lifeboat, men devouring each other in fear. But if he did not sound the alarm, eight hundred people would die in their sleep, slipping into a watery grave.

It was too much, and before the enormous possibilities he was powerless. Free, but powerless, and with nothing to fall back on, no traditions he could accept, no way of life that told him what to do, no instinctive response, because this he had given up. So he jumped—nowhere in particular with no thought but to block out a moment no man could handle.

But his fellow officers, with little imagination and no courage, had simply lowered a lifeboat and were quietly deserting the ship. And into their boat Jim fell, now part of their escape, part of a miserable world he had rejected, but which caught him up despite himself.

The next day the three are picked up, taken to Singapore and cashiered. Jim in disgrace retreats to a little island and lives with the natives; there he becomes Lord Jim—the great man of the island.

But the book is about two other men as well, about a French Navy officer who boards the ship the next day in obedience to orders. The *Patna* has not sunk after all and a French gunboat discovers her. The captain orders a line thrown to her and orders his lieutenant aboard.

The narrator asks him later why he did this. Did he not know the danger, could he not imagine the horror of the ship's sinking, still a possibility? But none of this means anything to him. He answers only that he must consider his honor. He must obey.

It is also about the British captain who presides over Jim's trial for desertion and sails for England, commanding a great liner—only to jump off the side of his ship in anticipation of the horror, in fear of the test that must come to him one day, too.

Conrad seems to be asking, Must we all be French lieutenants, dead and unimaginative, unaware and blind to survive in this world? Must we all do our duty and be protected by it, rather than live in freedom?

Is it inevitable that the man who thinks and feels and reacts to this world, who sees it for what it is, who stands in freedom before the great demands of life, must fail? Must he jump over the side of the ship because he cannot handle it? Must he retire into madness or drugs or alcohol and blot it all out?

Lord knows we cling to the tiniest things, the littlest movements, the tritest ideas to keep our hold on life, to protect ourselves from a world we cannot handle. Some say that is what the church is—that we have sold ourselves out to a miserable institution with all its pettifogging nonsense, its dull bureaucracy, its banality, in order to lose our freedom and be safe. Certainly many of us deny our freedom with narrow and frightened political convictions, by commitments to a host of bitter and frightened little groups that dot the landscape of American life. Too many of us are afraid to think and to feel and to face this exploding world, this crisis-ridden *Patna*.

At one point in my own life this was very serious, and I tried to deal with it in Jim's terms. He wanted total freedom, and total freedom became for him total slavery—because in the test he had nothing, nothing to hold to, nothing to support him. So I said to myself, Then a man must give up some of his freedom to keep the rest. But where can I give up freedom—even a small part of it—and be a man? And I looked around and nothing was worthy, nothing could be trusted. So I decided to give it up to God, who is not there, who only exists in the imagination of man, who is not present as the church is present, the state is present, the family is present.

Probably that is terrible theology, and I doubt that I could work it out even today—but I am sure there was some strange kind of truth there, some Pauline understanding that if God be my judge, then no man is my judge. If I stand free before my God, I stand free before all men.

So I have never really given up my freedom to the church and it is hardly the church I believe in. Though the Episcopal Church, to which I belong, in some measure is a curious kind of church which seems to have understood this freedom in some strange way. Its Catholic side has always said glorious things about bishops and the necessity of having them and obeying them—and then spends boundless energy denouncing one bishop or another, and as often as not disobeying him. While the Protestants have always thought that bishops were a little trivial, probably an inconvenience, but hardly a necessity—and then have proceeded to obey them. There was a moment in the nineteenth century when the Catholics were arguing the necessity of bishops—and the Protestants were sending them all over the world to head our missions.

It may be that if a man can make his commitments above and beyond or in and through the movements and institutions of his time, he then is free to deal with them, be part of them, yet always separate from them. But that is a terrifying freedom and we are not really up to it.

At the end of *Lord Jim*, the narrator listens to Jim's native wife. She asks him why Jim, the great man, Lord Jim, lives on this miserable little island. Why is he not in Singapore with the other white men? Why is he not building empires there? And the narrator answers brutally, "Because he is not good enough." But this is nonsense, says Jim's wife. Look at what he has done here. And the narrator reconsiders and answers, "Nobody, nobody is good enough." Nobody is good enough to be fully free, yet we are all too good to be slaves. How we deal with our freedom, then, may be the most basic question of all. Do we give our freedom to the state, to a man on a white horse, to a petty movement—or are we free to give it to God?

4

Four people spend the summer together on a deserted Swedish island: a father, his son, his daughter, and his daughter's husband. Each lives enclosed within himself—as far apart from each other and as barren within as the island is spacious and bleak without. And in that bleakness and separation, the daughter slowly goes mad. This is the story of Bergman's *Through a Glass Darkly*, like all his films, deeply involved with the Christian faith, preaching a richer and truer gospel than generally the church does—and speaking of the real nature of human suffering.

The girl slowly goes mad, and by the end of the film she is completely and brutally insane. And in her insanity she has a vision of a spider God, a monster deity coming to claim her for his own—perhaps her vision of a world, finally destructive, at its core madder than she is.

Each character reacts to her madness in his own way. The father and the son, drawn into it, horrified and terrified by it, become part of it and see their own bleakness, their own fear and hurt and sorrow, and come together. The film ends with the boy looking at the camera and saying, "My father talked to me." For the first time in his life his father spoke to him—and he heard him. For the first time out of the horror of the experience of his sister's madness he has confronted another person—and in the confrontation with her and his father begun to find himself. In some sense, then, these two have been saved by her madness.

The husband, however, the only one who is not alone, who has a relationship, who after all has a wife and then loses her, stays cool to the end. He stays removed and remote and kind and coldly compassionate. He loves his wife. He is the very picture of that affectless love, that immobile passion which starves the beloved and, by destroying love, makes of God a demon. At the end, confronted by the panic, the sheer terror of his wife, listening to her screams, he carefully and calmly opens his bag, pulls out a hypodermic and gives her a shot—untouched to the end. And as damned as she, he leaves the island to take her to the hospital.

The film is indeed dark, life seen and caught by reflections dimly perceived, as men struggle for life in the recesses of their minds and the darkness of their souls. But it is about hope and beauty as well. Because two men are saved. Two men find life and have a chance. Somewhere, somehow in the madness of the girl, they have found their savior.

It is almost as if Bergman knew better than Christians do the story of Thomas and his risen Lord. Thomas, who refuses to recognize Jesus except as the one who was always to be found among the pained, the hurt, the lost, sharing their hurt sharing their pain. He demands to see Jesus' wounds—only

a wounded Lord can be his savior; only a Lord who has passed
through the battles of this world can truly be resurrected.

The film is about the curious paradox of life found among
the dead, and joy among the wounded, of life for what it
really is, very painful, very hurtful, but possibly very beautiful
as well.

Because life is mixed, never pure, never unalloyed, and
that is what the story of Adam and Eve is about. Not about
the Garden of Eden or Adam and Eve in their purity—though
indeed it is a lovely image. Adam and Eve naked before each
other, and unafraid. Not only physically naked—the Bible is
never that shallow—but emotionally and spiritually naked.
Naked before each other because they are naked before
God. Therefore, they live in paradise, freely, openly and
without pain.

But this is not the world the story is about. The story deals
with the reality of Adam and Eve as you and me, as humanity
in this world. Because the story begins not at the beginning
but the end—the end, when Adam and Eve have been cast
out, when Eden is only a hope, in a world where men do
earn their bread by the sweat of the brow, where women
are lonely and afraid, and give birth in pain. The story begins
with a reality the author discerns and in his bones knows and
lives. It begins with Man—that is what "Adam" means in
Hebrew—alone in his world, knowing good and evil and torn
apart by that knowledge. Knowledge not as perception alone
—not the cool, detached knowledge of the Swedish doctor
watching his wife go mad, but the knowledge of a father
and son struggling with the madness of their daughter and
sister. Knowledge as involvement and relationship, not distant perception.

In Hebrew "knowledge" means "intimacy," and somewhere in the recesses of the Hebrew mind lurks the under-

standing that no one knows anything except as he has lived with it—no one knows a person except as he has loved or hated that person. So when Genesis speaks of Adam knowing Eve, this is not Victorian prudery unwilling to say that man and woman came together in sexual intercourse, but the beauty of the Hebrew mind saying that this is knowledge, for a man and woman to share and intertwine their bodies and the product of their bodies.

So the story of Adam and Eve is about the glory and the misery of man. It is about man knowing both good and evil. No longer in Eden, where he knew only God. But cast out of Eden, relating now to both God and the serpent, to both good and evil, and torn apart by that bitter knowledge. But free as well—because we can choose, because we are free to be captives to either. This is our humanity in all its tensions and torment—and all its hope.

Karl Marx, who also knew his Bible better than most of us, is the great historian of Adam. Because he speaks of man enslaved to greed, to economic determination, demanding to eat of the tree of the knowledge of good and evil every day, demanding to be God, to be master of other men. So Marx has a serious philosophy of history because he knows what drives history. He knows evil. But he does not really know good.

The Bible does. It knows Adam and Eve, and their torment. But it also knows God—and knows of the creator God caring for men and presenting another man before us to be our model and our hope. If Adam and Eve are the mirrors of man as he is caught between good and evil—then the Christ is the picture of man overcoming evil, obedient to good. And he is the free man, the man who in his freedom obeys God—and denies the serpent.

The Episcopal *Book of Common Prayer* contains a glorious

prayer that speaks of God "whose service is perfect freedom," a definition of God and of freedom beyond our im-
mediate experience, yet at the heart of any freedom at all
And the Holy Communion service the people of St. Mark's
wrote had a great blessing: Go: Serve the Lord. You are free.
And we knew it meant that you are free to serve him or not—
no one obeys the Lord or lives nobly except in freedom. And
we also knew that this is God's gift—freedom. The gift of the
world is slavery.

The New Testament begins with the strange story of a man
being baptized in the river Jordan—washing away his defilement, confessing therefore that he was a gentile in spirit
and not a Jew at all. Because the Jew needed no baptism. His
defilement, his uncleanness, his slavery was washed away in
the Red Sea in the crossing over that made him no longer a
slave but a free man before his Lord.

But this man Jesus, the Jew, went into the water to say
he was not clean, to associate himself with all the whores,
the pimps, the thieves, the scoundrels, the unwashed of the
earth—what the New English Bible calls in a strange kind of
eloquence "bad characters." He becomes one with the very
worst of life. He becomes earth and world and society and
man and intertwines himself with it all. He dies with it, so he
may rise with it.

I remember a baptism we once had at St. Mark's. A lovely
couple came to have their child baptized—but the god-
parents were unbelievably stuffy and so were some of the
friends. So I preached a little sermonette about baptism. I
began by saying how lovely it was that we were gathered
together here to make an Episcopalian of this little girl. And
everybody beamed. Because everybody knew what that im-
plied—status in a WASP world. And everybody but the
parents wanted that for the child—entrance into the world of

Episcopal manners, as one of them put it to me, the world of getting ahead and making the right connections.

But I went on to say that is not really what we are doing. We are saying in this service that this child is potentially a whore, potentially lost, really dead, really drowned in the waters until the Lord calls her forth and gives her life. Some of the people, I guess, wished they had not come—wished they had not been given their own chance to deal with life.

The one who went into the water originally is also the one who descended into the very depths of human experience, who finally died a brutal death on the cross. Not just because all death is brutal—though it is and it is no good to romanticize it. But because this death was especially brutal. It was so determined by executioner and executed. One of the eloquent substatements of the passion is Jesus' refusal to accept the narcotic offered him on the cross. It would have dulled his pain, dulled his experience of the moment—and made it easier for the executioners to avoid the moment, too, to say to themselves, We have not been brutal. We have indeed been merciful. We dulled his pain.

He must die painfully and fully if he is to live for all those whose deaths were equally brutal, whose lives were oppressed and hurt and destroyed. So he descends into hell.

John Calvin, stiff and unbending though he was, knew life, and knew enough to know what the descent into hell means. The great cry from the cross, "My God, my God, why have you forsaken me," is the descent into hell. There is no deeper hell for man than brutal aloneness—no deeper hell than to confront God as a spider, as a monster, as a demon.

Jesus descended into hell, and there, says the New Testament, he discovered the gates of heaven. That is very curious and very complex thinking, and even more difficult experiencing, because that is what is required—every man's descent into hell to discover the gates of heaven.

The Old Testament knew the story before it ever happened. It knew the story as basic to human existence. Jacob, the scoundrel, the cheat, but the father of his people, wrestled with the angel one night. He wrestled with his own soul and his future—and in the morning the angel threw him to the ground, dislocated his hip, and gave him a new name: Israel, which means in Hebrew "he who struggles with God." And when the angel threw him and when he finished his struggle, he discovered the gates of heaven before him with angels ascending and descending, with the very heavens coming to him to greet him and welcome him to this new world which in his struggle he had discovered.

We are God's people if we struggle with him, if we throw ourselves into the life he made for us, if we accept what it is and call out to him to wrestle. It is as if man goes into the depths in order to scale the heights. Jesus goes down into the river Jordan and comes up out of the waters to hear the voice of the Lord say: "You are my chosen one, with you I am well pleased."

The Lord says he is well pleased with one whose being is all wrapped up with creation, all wrapped up with good and evil, with the depths and heights of life, who is all of life, every part of it, not just some parts of it, neither the good parts alone, nor the bad parts. The one with whom God is well pleased is the one who is all wrapped up with his brothers, who knows that what happens to them happens to him.

Years ago an Episcopal priest named John Harmon wrote of his ministry in the black ghetto of Boston. He said he was sitting in his office one day congratulating himself on his incarnational ministry. For ten years he had been among them, among the blacks. And he thought back on all those days when he, a blond, blue-eyed product of Ivy League colleges and the WASP world, had given of himself to those people.

And he opened up John's gospel to reread the story of the incarnation on which he based his ministry only to see that Jesus had never gone among *them*—among some other people—but among his own. And John Harmon said that day he knew that he had lost ten years of his life in an illusion—that he had not really lived out the incarnation, and never could until he accepted the people around him as his own, one with every man who stands by his side.

There was a vestryman at St. Mark's whom I loved very dearly, an old Southern conservative who had laid his life on the line for freedom long before I ever dared to do it, who said to me: "Preacher, if you ever use that word 'them,' I'll stand up in the middle of the sermon and call you out for it. There is no 'them' or 'they' in this world, just 'us.'"

Life is not "us" and "them." There are no "thems" or "theys," only "us," messing up our common lives, sharing our common disasters, slaves with the slaves, free with the free. The man Christ, who makes himself one with all men, with the very worst of society, dies on the cross and is raised up by the only life-giving power there is, to be alive for all men now and any other time that we want to be alive.

I am not sure I understood this when I came to St. Mark's any better than John Harmon did. But before I could think about it, before I could struggle loose, I was caught in the grip of a depressed and hurt and lost community, and I was depressed, and I have known ever since that my freedom is all tied up with the freedom of my people, of the people with whom I share the struggle to be. We have been in the depths together. Somehow we will share the heights.

John Robinson knows the truth when he denies a God out there, in the great beyond, waiting to be called into our problems or our hurts. The New Testament knows no such God. I know no such God. The Bible takes God for granted as being with us—a mystery in our midst, never leaving us, never apart.

Dietrich Bonhoeffer talks of men searching for the unknown beyond the known—looking into the stars and the great beyond, and not knowing that the unknown is always to be found precisely in the midst of the known, and not somewhere else.

The New Testament talks about the hiddenness of God which is found in life, in living life with all its complexities and its doubts and anxieties. The call to be sensitive, to feel, is a call to be alive, to share your feelings with your fellowmen—and among us all to find life.

I remember once in a mental hospital a patient explaining his problem. He drew a circle on the table—and kept drawing it with his finger as he said, "That's them—always together, always together." And then he withdrew his finger and far away from the circle made a little dot, and said, "That's me, always alone, never together." And I felt very sad for him, and I still do. But I also knew how angry he was at everyone else —at all the "theys" of this world who were destroying him. But he was destroying himself, standing apart from life, unwilling to throw himself in to receive the gift.

Martin Luther once said that Jesus Christ was not God stalking the earth, being Godlike. But that God was present "in, with, by, under, and through" the man Jesus. Just as he is present "in, with, by, under, and through" the bread and wine of the Mass—just as he is present "in, with, by, under, and through" the moment in which you live.

You will never see God. You will never live apart from the world with God. And if you search for him to love you, to sustain you and then reject your fellowmen in the process, you have denied him. He is not to be found stalking the earth, but precisely in the moment, among the people you love and who love you. Never to be equated with the moment, never to be equated with anybody—but to be known "in, with, by, under, and through" the moment, the person.

The question is whether a man can see and feel and know the depths of life, whether he is willing to risk taking that plunge into the fullness of man, of humanity. So the term "Son of Man" in the New Testament is a Hebrew term for "fully man," for "intensified man," for "What a man!" The search for freedom, the search for truth is the search for our own humanity—and nothing is as serious as this: a man, the man. Me and You.

The story of Adam and Eve is the story of men and women as they are in truth, now, struggling with life. The story of the Son of Man, of Jesus the Christ, is the story of man as he will be, as he is becoming, you and me as we grow into the fullness of the stature of the Son of Man.

But I have met very few Christians who can deal with Jesus Christ in classic terms, who can say easily that he is the son of God. And I wonder if we need to say that, if we need to use terms that have nothing to do with our own experience.

All I can say is that this concern with one man in history is a concern for all men in history. If you are concerned with this one man in his one moment of time, in his one place of living, then you are concerned with every man in every time in every place. If that one moment in history is precious, every moment is precious.

You and I can speak pretty glibly about the preciousness of human life and the inherent nobility of man—and not know why we believe it or if we do at all. As long as we believe that in any sense at all something weird and mysterious and beautiful happened around 30 A.D., that somehow then a man, a beautiful man, triumphed over death in every moment of his life—and on the cross—and lived victoriously as well on the streets of Palestine as from the grave, then we have endowed every moment in history with the same potential—and every man.

This story about the man does not define fully what it means to be a man. You and I are going to have to find that out for ourselves. Nor does it say what we will do with our freedom: only what he did with his. But it is the promise that we can be men, that we can work out our freedom, that death is not the final answer. It is the promise that it is worth trying to be human.

At the heart of the Judeo-Christian tradition stands our conviction that the gates of heaven are on this earth and that what happens on this earth is of ultimate importance. The truth can in some sense be known. Men can be human.

But this depends on a church that is concerned with the creator God, not with its own God, its petty deity, the deity of religion and goodness. And it depends on people who are pleased to be dragged into the struggle in order to find themselves.

We put on a play once at St. Mark's that did more to destroy me—and then build me—than any work of art ever has, I suppose. We were just beginning Theatre Genesis and we had promised a theatre of freedom where new playwrights could work out their art and work out their humanity.

The director, Ralph Cook, came up to see me on vacation and showed me the first play he wanted to do, *Rock Garden*, a play by a twenty-year-old named Sam Shepard—now one of the great hopes of the American theatre, whose work has reached Broadway.

I read the play and I almost passed out. I asked Ralph if we had to begin with this one. Could we not start with something milder and less drastic? I had visions of the *Daily News* headlining the morning edition with "Smut at St. Mark's."

And I was convinced the vice squad would close the play down. It was a terrible moment, which got progressively worse until the play opened—and then it shocked me to the very core of my being.

The play opens with a mother, a terrible nagging, griping mother, lying in bed covered with blankets, snuffling with a cold in her head and complaining—endlessly complaining. Next to her on a chair sits a young man who we assume is her son. He has nothing on but his undershorts and he is listening in silence to the endless assault—as Mother rattles on for the whole first scene.

She asks him to go get her a glass of water, and he does, coming back with pants on. He gets her another glass of water and comes back with a shirt. By the end of the first scene he is muffled up in a navy pea jacket—protected from his mother's assaults.

It is not altogether clear what Mother is saying. Her words make little sense. But much of the new theatre and the new art is not about words anyway. It is total experience. And I sat in my seat with the same revulsion the young man felt.

Suddenly the father appears—and the son leaves and the mother rolls over in bed and turns her back on him.

In the second scene, the father appears on stage with socks and garters, underpants and undershirt and hat, with a can of beer in hand—and belches. He sits down. The son is sitting away from him on a stool. And the father begins his assault—a little like a pneumatic jackhammer busting concrete. His words make as little sense as Mother's at first and then gradually begin to open up. He is talking about his rock garden, about the rocks he collects and piles up around the watering pipes in the garden, and the little bits of vegetation that grow around the sprinkler heads in the rocks. The words begin to make some kind of sense if you know Freud, if you share with all of America a repressed sexuality and erotic vision.

All during the father's speech the son sits in his chair recoiling before what his father says, and falling off at intervals. Then the father stops talking and the son begins.

He speaks with a kind of soft and tender beauty, from the depths of a young and growing spirit. The sounds are pure and rhythmic, and they wake up the audience, as if it were morning and we had just discovered the freshness of the dew. But the words reveal the most thoroughly pornographic speech I have ever heard. It is as if the son were breaking every taboo of our society—using every dirty word, conjuring up every repressed image—and laying them out before his father as his gift—of life. And the play ends with the father falling off his chair.

At every performance people got up in horror and left sometimes silently, sometimes very noisily. Something inside of me tried to get up and leave, but could not. Instead, I sat there assaulted, ready to fall off my chair, and rethinking my own existence.

It would be obvious to say that it was a play about the failure of communications between young and old—and probably untrue. They communicated only too well, but without words, denying their emotions. Rather it seemed to be about the great whited sepulcher which too often passes for life.

Mother and Father speaking the king's English, living up to all the proprieties, being good people, and underneath the most unbelievable dirt, death and bones and corruption and decay, every action and every word revealing the whited sepulcher. But the son listening to his parents, somehow freeing himself of them, being alive in feeling and sensitivity and experience, tells his parents, I am going to live with your death words—and leave you to die with your so-called life words.

Maybe Sam Shepard at twenty had to tell us again that out of death, out of the things we fear, the moments of terror, the facts we cannot accept, what we believe to be evil, comes life. So it is a resurrection play in a very curious and special kind of way—the mother and father destroying their son, dragging him into their world of death—and the son rising to life with beauty and warmth and hope.

As I understand the Gospel story, the heart of Christian feeling and thinking, it speaks of the possibility of a man descending into the Jordan and rising into life. It is possible to live his life with whores, pimps, thugs, and all the rest. It is possible for a man to taste of evil, to be part of it, to be imbued with it as we all are and at the same time to rise and be a man and find beauty.

This is what Martin Luther meant by sinning boldly. Martin Luther, no more than St. Paul, was encouraging people to go out and rub their noses in the dirt. No man needs to duplicate Genet's life to find whatever sainthood some ascribe to this strange and perverse French playwright and author who used the desperation of his own soul and his own actions as the soil from which to produce some great and tender beauty. But Luther did understand that no man lives without sin, without profound sin, both in himself, in his own soul, and in the world he shares with other men.

Therefore sin boldly—risk the sin, risk the evil, which must come anyway—and try to live as courageously and fully as you can.

We cannot divide the world into us and them, church and nonchurch, Christians and unbelievers, black and white. If we divide the world into good and evil and think we are good, we are not really alive at all, because somehow we have tried to evade what we truly are: a part of the very primeval chaos with which the Lord wrestles every day, wrenching from it life and meaning and order.

At the heart of Christianity is this assertion: Jesus Christ is the one who is not afraid to be free, not afraid to obey and go into the depths of human existence, sharing life with all men —to wait there to be called out.

How that works out for each of us is what the rest of life is about. But first I think we have to believe this. Otherwise wait and pray for someone to come along and shock you and shove you kicking and screaming into the mainstream of life where first you will taste what it means to be alive.

5

My theological education really began at McSorley's Old Ale House. And I still go back as often as I can to continue and deepen and never lose hold of what I learned there in the oldest Irish ale house in New York. It is a lovely place, sawdust on the floor, an old potbellied stove in the center of the front room, old wood tables with a century's worth of initials carved into the tops, and the very best beer you can get in New York. Old men sit all day in the sunlight that comes through the front windows and sip their ale, and a family of cats romps through the sawdust taking in the sweet smells of ale and onions and cheese. And there they practice the oldest of all discriminations, no women allowed, even though the owner is a woman. There is some deep irony there that I do not understand, but then I have never really understood the Irish at all—even though they taught me what

I needed to know about Christianity and taught it to me at McSorley's.

One day I went into McSorley's, just another day like many before, except that I had just been elected rector of St. Mark's in the Bowery. As I walked in, the bartender looked at me and banged his mug on the bar for silence. And then in a rich baritone called out, "Set 'em up for the new rector of our parish!" That really threw me—this Irish bartender welcoming me, the Anglican, as the new rector of the parish. What on earth was he saying to me?

I thought I knew something about the Irish. Somewhere back in the eighteenth century my Allen ancestor had arrived here from Ireland, from County Wexford, and he had been a priest of the Anglican Church of Ireland. He came with his wife and his wife's sister and his wife's first cousin, and as each died, he married the next, one of the few men to arrive in the new world thoroughly prepared for its rigors and deprivations. But I also had a great-aunt who was considerably more Irish than Cardinal O'Boyle, the only Irish Catholic in my thoroughly Protestant family. She had always been very fond of me and used to tell me of my renegade Methodist grandfather who had married a renegade Irish Catholic, her sister, and how much her family had worried about their souls' health. But when I decided to become an Episcopal priest and go to the Episcopal Theological School in Cambridge, Massachusetts, everything changed. I got a letter from Aunt Mabel, bordered in black, telling me that I had betrayed my heritage. I had gone over to them (the English), therefore henceforth I would be dead in her eyes, and that is exactly the way it has been ever since. My wife and I tried writing to her once in a while. We sent Christmas cards for a few years. But no reply, ever. I had committed the great betrayal. So the bartender broke into a private world and threw

me completely off center by the very thought that I could be
rector of an Irish bartender's parish. And this meant some research into my native land and into my spiritual roots.

The seventeenth-century Church of Ireland was a rare and
beautiful and horrible thing. It believed that the rector of the
parish was responsible for the life, welfare, hope, dignity, and
joy of every man and woman in the parish—and only sec-
ondarily for the people of the church congregation. This ex-
cluded no one and allowed for no inner circle, no smaller
body. And by extension the church congregation was responsible for the life and welfare of everyone in the parish. It
occurs to me how far we have strayed from that ideal, how
far we now are with exclusive parish churches that do not
minister to their people, that do not care about their communities, that accept tax exemptions and offer nothing to the
community that granted them but stale and dreary services
with pious and irrelevant sermons.

But I also discovered something else. The rector of that
parish church was called "parson," except it is not spelled
that way at all, but really "person"—the person of the parish,
the man set aside to work out his humanity, the fullness of
what it means to be a man in this time, this place. And it
never means the same thing everywhere or in every time. It is
always different in every parish in every age. The person, the
man who works out his humanity for others, for the sake of
all those people whose health and welfare he must serve,
not by doing things for them, not by giving them free gifts
or admonishing them to goodness, but by living out his life
in a way everyone else could live out his, that life which is
always mixed with pain and sorrow, joy and laughter. And if
this is so, then of course the function of the church is the
same, to work out the life of that community in a manner
that could apply to the parish around it, to work out the

tensions and the bitternesses, the selfishness and the greed, so that somehow in forgiveness and understanding, in compassion and love, we might live together and not destroy each other, but create something of beauty in our midst. But always in this time and in this place.

And the more diverse the parish, the more real the experience of working out humanity. Because the image of God is not a man, but men—all men in their diversity and their difference, black and white, yellow and brown, with all their languages and their cultures and their confusions. The image of God is man and woman, young and old. Protestant and Catholic, Jew and agnostic and atheist. In the midst of the confusion and the diversity the parson-person tries to work out his humanity as a coherent response to the humanity of those around him, so that they in turn may do the same with him and with that congregation of Christians who seek to take community seriously if only for a brief moment, if only in the heart of worship.

This was so exciting to discover, to discover that the church really could have greater meaning than its denominationalism and sectarianism, that we are not called to form men into stereotypes, or to fill pews and pay church bills, but somehow to enhance the humanity of men. And then I discovered that the Church of Ireland was no better than the rest. It, too, had failed its purpose—or denied it. For when the English conqueror came to Ireland, he set up his parish church and turned his back on the people, and served instead the English squire and his lady. The parson related only to the English, working out only a narrow humanity, ignoring the people and driving them away. And it is important to know that the seventeenth-century Irish were prepared to follow the English into the Reformation and leave Rome behind—but not after they saw the English church with all its pretensions and its shabby performance. So they went back to Rome with a vengeance and a bitterness with which we still live and which poisoned my relationship with an aunt I loved, and who I think loved me.

The bartender had called me to justify my own past, to live up to my ideals and his, to offer once again a chance, a possibility that the Christian church could offer humanity to all the people, and not repression and not contempt and not indifference. He had his bitter memories and I had mine. We all do, and somewhere in all our past lurks that Church of Ireland parish, ministering to the lord and lady and ignoring the people.

One of my friends told me once of his curacy at a great and historic church, built for the *nouveau riche,* dominated still by those who put position and power above compassion and concern. One day he had visited with the tired old rector, a beautiful man who had stayed too long and broken his heart among a people whom he had tried to love. Looking around at the pictures on the walls of his study, pictures of former rectors who had become bishops of the church, and among them some of the great men of the Episcopal Church, he said, "Do you realize that those men there and you and I and every man who ever served this church have been lackeys, nothing but lackeys to lick the boots of the men who called us here to serve them?" The story almost broke my heart as I imagined that lovely old man called not to be a man, but a lackey, called not to find a common humanity that would bind together a community, but called to protect privilege and ignorance and contempt.

But this has long been our story. Think of how many churches and faiths we have created by our unwillingness to love the people. Think of the ponderous medieval papacy fanning the flames of reformation. Martin Luther never wanted to leave the Church—only to love the people and serve their needs for humanity. But the incredible stupidity of a blind papacy drove him out. And the Anglicans drove out the Methodists, who had found a "method" to meet the needs of eighteenth-century men. Wesley to his dying day was a priest of the Church of England—but banished from communion with his fellow Anglicans. And think of the Harlem Protestants who created the Black Muslim movement by rejecting the poor and turning their backs on their own brethren when they came crying for help, lost in their identities, looking for manhood. Maybe now we have created Timothy Leary and the Woodstock Nation because we are not aware or do not care about a generation around us looking deeply for identity and meaning in life. And the church again turns its back on the best in its tradition to affirm the narrowest sectarianism it can find.

So I accepted the challenge and I decided I would try to be a seventeenth-century Irish parson, that I would begin there. And I knew that would make me a modernist among some of my brethren who may be several centuries behind me. I thought I could be the parson for this parish, this screwy, impossible Lower East Side to which I had been called. Perhaps I could help form St. Mark's as a church for others that could live for its parish.

Now I know why I was called to that parish. The suffragan bishop told me just in case I overlooked it. He said St. Mark's had always been a screwy parish and it had always called screwy rectors—and he thought I maintained the tradition. And I suppose I do. I looked out over the parish of St. Mark's and realized it was the most diverse and complex and impossible place you could ever think of. The Lower East Side is made up of every fragment of the human race that you can imagine, all of them fearing each other, as men are basically wont to do, unable to find any unity in their diversity, and then I looked at my own background and how well it fitted the parish. I was born in France of a renegade Methodist mother, and a would-be Irish Catholic father who never really had anything to do with any faith, raised in good, sound Methodist territory in Oregon, lived on Washington Square in New York, college in Boston, graduate school in France. There has never been any unity in my own soul, and so perhaps I belong in a place where men are struggling to find some way to hold together and not collapse in confusion.

This meant that the congregation of St. Mark's and I had to find our identity as human beings in this strange place, now, and nowhere else. And that meant I could not go into the parish as a Christian hero to minister to "them." I cannot even give of myself for others unless first I see the people of the Lower East Side as my brothers and sisters and am willing to immerse myself in their life and make it mine. Unless I do that, I do not know what the Incarnation is about.

When I first went to St. Mark's in 1959, the depression that I had always carried within me began to be really serious, and it has lasted in some sense ever since. And one of the key words in the congregation has been "depression." We talk about it and feel it because the Lower East Side is the most depressed community I have ever known. And no one can live there without being caught in it and becoming part of that depression.

The Lower East Side is famous in American history as the place people have left. People have gone there involuntarily and then have left: Eddie Cantor left the Lower East Side. The great American sculptor Jo Davidson left the Lower East Side. Our respected senior senator from New York, Jacob Javits, left the Lower East Side and only returns once in a while

to gather some votes and eat a knish. Nobody stays on the
Lower East Side if he can leave.

When I first came to the parish, my black friends did not
really live there. They had addresses there, but they did not
live there. Everybody I knew lived somewhere else. My black
friends all lived in Brooklyn or Harlem or wherever they had
come from and where they spiritually remained. They could
not face the thought of living in this dreadful community and
living out its depression.

I remember walking down Second Avenue nine or ten
years ago. What a depressing experience that was. A street
coming apart—the lifeline of a community with no life.
Shabby stores and shabby people and long faces reflecting a
community of rejects. A community of all the unwashed and
the unwanted. It used to be the Jews, the first great immigra-
tion. And there are still Jews left, mostly the old folks who
have been left behind to die. And the Slavs. The community
is full of Poles and Ukrainians. And now the artists and the
blacks and the Puerto Ricans and the hippies. The people nobody really wants. The people for whom we build ghettos. Do
not forget that we want our artists and intellectuals around no
more than we want our blacks and Puerto Ricans. We are all
rejects of a society whose standards encompass narrow virtues and small ideals and even smaller hopes. We send off our
black people to win Olympic medals and then stick them back
in the ghetto, and we ask our artists to paint great pictures to
put in the Museum of Modern Art, and then send them back
to the ghetto because nobody wants an artist around the
house.

Be careful lest we ignore George Wallace, or the men who
will follow him, who build their careers on the bitterness of
the disenfranchised. George Wallace was very popular among
the Slavs of the Lower East Side. He has made up a movement

of people nobody wants, and they want their revenge, as rightly they should have it. People who are rejected and hurt and spat upon are going to be angry people, bitter people. They cannot be beautiful. They are very likely to be ugly. And nobody has ever defended the Slavs of the Lower East Side. The word "Polack" has been around almost as long as some of the other words we use to destroy men's dignity and humanity. And such a man hates everything he thinks holds him in tyranny. He hates the intellectuals, the hippies, the commies, the blacks, all those real or imagined people who threaten his existence. And if he makes it out of the Lower East Side to Queens or Brooklyn, then he has to hang on to what little he has achieved and hold off the enemy, those as rejected as he is, as hurt as he is, crying for the same manna.

And the hippies. Even though the hippies are the sons and daughters of the rich, of WASPs, they are unwanted, too. Do not kid yourself about the flower children in that brief moment when they flourished on the Lower East Side. Their parents had never wanted them—their parents who found them basically a bother as they climbed up the ladder of social success or traveled the martini circuit. They sent their children away to boarding school or just sent them into the bedroom to be ignored. And so they had to build a world for themselves. And for a while it was a world of flowers and fantasy. And the Lower East Side murdered a flower girl and it all went bad, and the fantasy went away and was replaced by ugly reality.

I remember the time the Up Against the Wall Motherfuckers (MFs for short) announced that they wanted to have a series of meetings at St. Mark's. They were about the most unattractive band of roving youths I have ever known. They had no apparent purpose, except to live on the street, gathering together the street people, the runaways, the depressed, the lost, playing on their fears and bitternesses. I was willing to let them meet, because we had decided any community group could meet in the parish hall at least once. Except that they wanted to meet on the Wednesday nights when the poets had regularly scheduled readings. Wednesday night was special to the MF's, because it was on a Wednesday they had liberated the Fillmore East. They broke up a rock performance there and demanded a free night for the community to produce its own music. They had been right in what they did, because the Fillmore, like the church, had an obligation to put something back into the community. But they soon forgot this liberation and now had wandered off to something else. The MF spokesman told me that he had more right to the parish hall than the poets did because his cause mattered and was right and there were more MFs than poets. And I thought I heard faint echoes of a bank president father telling his son about the rights of the rich and the washed in a land of the poor and the unwashed.

So we had a confrontation with the MFs, angry children who had never worked out anything with their parents. I told their leader they could try to destroy the church and take me on. That was all right. But they could not take on the poets, their brothers and sisters—who had as many rights as they did. And when they did, it was shotgun time for me. It is very late when you are thirty, as their leader was, to work things out with your parents, much harder than when you are ten and life is still in its formative stages.

But the blacks and the Puerto Ricans hated the hippies for giving up what they had never had, for giving up wealth and social acceptance and mobility. And they did not know how much these were all illusions. Maybe now they have grown to understand better our common deprivations, and as we all grow sadder and more oppressed, perhaps we grow wiser.

So the Lower East Side is full of violence. When I first came into the community, we had almost nightly gang fights in Tompkins Square. One night the Italian gang cut up a Puerto Rican boy. The next night the Puerto Rican gang doubled the damage on an Italian boy. And so it went night after night.

Then Mobilization for Youth came into the community, not because we were the most violent in the city, but because violence was mounting at a more rapid rate. What a price we pay for listening to the serpent and preferring him to that other voice. It does ugly things to a man to be rejected and to be hurt, and there are really only two outlets for all that hurt, either depression or anger. Anger is a healthy and beautiful thing if it is free to destroy ugliness and build beauty, but if the forces of repression are great enough, then depression is all that is left. And into such a mess came MFY. They discovered that in the first year of their life, I think it was 1961, more kids had died from overdoses of drugs than from gang warfare in the entire preceding ten years. So they looked into the growth of addiction and the decline of gang warfare, and found some fascinating and horrible truths. Gang warfare was subsiding because the repression had been so enormous. The police and the courts had come in so hard and with such violence on the bopping gangs that overt anger, that action of any kind, was impossible and only depression remained. And the answer to that is drugs and escape into a world of fantasy where men and women smile at each other and kiss and make up, and everybody loves everyone else and all men are equal.

This is what the parson has to deal with, not from the outside, not from a distance or a place of holiness, but from the inside, and that means getting depressed himself, feeling the agony of the people, sharing it in some manner, and trying to find a way out, a way out that works for him and for the people. So it seemed right to call a depressive kind of rector if that is the kind of community you have and if the church and the parson are willing to share in the life of the people. Because then they can try to respond to the call which brings men up out of the depths; they can try to live in the midst of death.

In a curious kind of way maybe the parson has to risk losing his identity as a man so that with his people, together, they may find a new identity, and that may be a way of talking about the life which is only seen through the cross.

I know this is why Martin Luther has always fascinated me so much, because I can think of no man in Western history more haunted, insecure, hurt, and afraid, a man who was almost and sometimes totally psychotic, whose search for identity was so desperate. But this man in his terrible lostness matched the lostness and confusion of his time; he mirrored in some strange way the lostness of the people he lived among and served. And finding his identity meant in some way the finding of the identity of all his people, and of Western European man.

Erik Erikson talks about Luther in these terms in *The Young Man Luther*. It is a very troubling and disturbing kind of book. He says in his preface that he wrote it as his gift to the troubled and creative young people with whom he has worked all his life. But he wanted to write not a series of case histories, but the case history of one of the most troubled young men of all time who is also one of our greatest men. He wanted to write in the context of hope. It is about the search for identity and the crisis of identity; it is about a man so troubled, so insecure that he cared enough to find a whole new meaning in life. He took upon himself the very identity struggles of his fellow Germans and their transition from feudalism to the city and the life of the burgher and the kind of freedom and independence this required. *The Freedom of the Christian Man* is the great work of Martin Luther because he was a slave himself, a slave to incredible darkness in his own soul, who had to find freedom for himself. He was a great pastor. He was a great parson because he knew and loved the people he served and therefore he created a new church for them and for himself.

As Erikson says, here was a man who demanded in his own soul commitment to something great, something beyond himself, something rich and beautiful and right. But there was nothing worthy of his commitment. So he had to find a truth, re create a faith, reform Christianity so he could believe it and commit himself to it—and therefore to the Lord of that faith. I think back on Lord Jim, a man who also needed commitment, the man of our own time who is reaching out for something to believe and to obey, when nothing is in sight, nothing is worthy of his belief. Conrad juxtaposed Lord Jim with the French lieutenant who found his commitment in the French Navy, and what a terrible God that is, how small and tight and finally vicious. He found his commitment to honor, and that is one of the lesser virtues. St. Paul suggested that after all personal integrity is not the greatest goal of all. The real goal for man is concern for the church, concern for the community, concern for the building of the body of Christ, for the enhancing of the common humanity. And when a man can find nothing to give himself to and nothing to believe, then he knows it is today, when politically, socially, religiously there is nothing that really demands me and dignifies me in the demand. The Almost Chosen People cannot do that for me. An American flag as the symbol of a nation that has not lived up to its dreams, and has denied its best values, can hardly be my commitment.

Luther in his most desperate moments would repeat to himself like a constant litany, "I have been baptized, I have been baptized." And this kept him from madness, the belief that even in his own darkness and even though he could find no direction, somebody was calling to him and evoking new life in the very midst of his crisis.

There is a beautiful story of Luther being lost in a dark and terrible depression for a month, locked in his room, seeing no one, accepting food from his wife, Katie, but neither speaking to her nor really seeing her. And then one day he walked out of his room, ready to enter the arena again and with the manuscript of *A Mighty Fortress Is Our God* in hand.

Maybe the parson and the church, if they are willing to sink into the depths of that community and share the rejection of the rejected and the hurt of the hurt, may at last be ready to hear the call and start moving out for the Promised Land. And they could dance. They could dance to a tune sung by a great lion who even now is creating his world anew and afresh. That is something to live for and that is something that hauls a man out of his depression, his sadness, and his loneliness and makes him human.

6

We had an art show in the parish hall and the women of the altar guild went to look at it with me, and with a rare kind of unity they all told me how much they hated it. Every single member of the altar guild was angry to the roots of her being, absolutely furious. I had seen very little of that beautiful passion in them before, and how gloriously alive they all were that day. Clearly no one could ever accuse the artist of failing to move the people. Most of the paintings were the work of Aldo Tambolleni, a very strange and angry man, beautiful in his way, but compelled to deny that beauty in himself and compelled as if by a demon to destroy the love men had for him. He was so angry and so hurt. It is curious how those things go together, anger and hurt. He was out to destroy everything and anything he could find in order to create, and he could almost get away with it, his genius was so enormous. He was an artist of the revolution in many ways. Most of his paintings were great black circles on white, all kinds of circles, big and little circles, all of them angry circles. You have no idea how much a black circle can express until you have seen Aldo's circles. They enraged everyone. It almost turned us into snarling animals. And the floor of the parish hall was littered with tortured cement sculpture, ragged, jagged hunks of cement with spikes sticking out of them. There were rusted car wheels and all sorts of street junk piled into the cement, and these, too, made us all angry.

I tried to explain that we were all angry because the art was angry, because Aldo was angry, because he was trying to provoke a response in us. He was trying to make us angry and trying to make us do something about our anger. That is why he was a revolutionary artist. He was trying to make something happen inside a man so he could be more aware of himself, so he would want to change the world and make it beautiful—so someday he could take away the great black angry circles and create instead a lovely pastoral scene which would be the truth about life. Because of his own deep anguish, I doubt that Aldo Tambolleni will ever paint a pastoral scene, but we could think about it and what would be required to do it. But that made the altar guild even angrier, so we dropped the discussion for that day.

A little bit later some of the black kids of the parish came in. They were all from Avenue D and the housing projects by the East River. I asked them to look around and think about the art and tell me how they felt. One of the kids took a long look at the cement hulk with its nails and old wheels and said, "It looks like a battleground. Everybody is getting killed."

And another guy said, "Yeah, just like Avenue D, 'cause you know he picked that junk up off the street." Those kids really understood Aldo. These were street scenes, these cement sculptures. They were scenes of the battleground where these kids live and where Aldo lives. But Aldo was trying to give that battleground and those streets some kind of form, some kind of shape and substance. He was really involved in creating, in pulling meaning out of chaos. He was involved in the great and essential creative act, but the kids had trouble understanding that. They had trouble dealing with that battleground and making sense out of it. They were not yet artists, not yet free enough to transcend the horror of those streets.

I remember telling the kids one day about an experience I had had the night before, coming home from the movies with my wife. I saw a struggle going on on the corner. A man was wrestling with a young woman, and a group of big tough men were standing around, looking very menacing, very ready to jump in and kill the man. I knew there was going to be real trouble and I moved over closer. Then I saw that the man had a pistol and it was still in its holster, strapped under his arm. Only policemen carry holsters and guns like that. And suddenly I realized this was a policeman trying to make an arrest, and he was scared. Whether he was right or wrong, someone was going to get killed if he did not get out of there fast. So I volunteered to help and he asked me to put his handcuffs on the girl. I did, and he took her away and the men did nothing. I never saw the cop again and I do not know what happened or what the scene was really about.

The kids were furious. How could I help a cop! They were absolutely incensed. And I tried to explain that life cannot be a perpetual battleground, with brutal deaths and constant violence. I tried to explain that I did not want to see anyone killed that night. And I knew how scared the cop was and how likely it was that he would shoot, and then it would be too late. One of those men would be dead, and maybe the cop or the girl would be dead, too. And I did not want to see that happen. But that is the chaos in which we all are living, which we could hardly wrench ourselves out of. And Aldo had touched it somehow and worked it into art, which is, I think, the beginning of what it means to be a man, to be able to shape your experience into some kind of meaning. To take your experience of life seriously. And how very few of us do take our experience seriously, and therefore deny our own humanity before we have even formed it.

I remember a Saturday night one winter when I had to write a sermon on the Marriage Feast at Cana. After eleven years as a priest, I finally confessed that I really did not know what that story was about. I did not understand it and I had never understood it. I had read every commentary and thought what they all said was interesting, but they really meant nothing to me. So I faced my own confusion and the recognition that I had nothing to say to the people. Then my mind began to wander and I thought about wine. I thought about the summer we had just spent in Europe and the month we had driven around France. The evenings had been so lovely. My wife and children and I stopped in little French hotels all around the country, and ate dinner together, those long, glorious French dinners, with lots of wine. And everywhere we went the wine was different. Sometimes full and rich, like Burgundy. I thought of the little town we had stayed in, with a church on top of a hill, looking out over rich and beautiful fields. And a restaurant across the square from the church where a big-boned peasant woman served us dinner. Sausages and vegetables and then beef in wine. A full, rich meal served by full, rich people, and with it, a Burgundy reflecting all the strength and power of that richest part of France. But I also remembered the night we spent near Verdun, near the great battlefields of World War I. And the wine there was a rosé, but not even really rosé, just gray and thin, like a people who have lost too much blood, who have seen too many deaths and too many wars. And I thought about wine as a kind of reflection of life. How could I preach about that? About a summer in France with my wife and children? And then I caught myself. What on earth am I doing to myself, denying my own experience, the only really precious thing I have to offer anyone? Because it is in my experience of life that the Lord speaks, not in some other place or time. So it turned out that one of the best sermons I ever preached was on wine, on all that wine means to me, and maybe therefore to other men. I had made my own experience part of the creative act.

We had a great sculpture hanging from a tree in the yard one year. People went by and laughed at it, and the garbage men would stop and offer to take it away. Some people even got angry at it and threatened to cut it down from the tree— or cut down the tree if necessary. But nobody ignored it; nobody could, because it was made out of wrecked cars, blue fenders and red doors and yellow wheels, and chrome bumpers from smashed cars. Here was the stuff of the carnage of our highways, real stuff of death and destruction, but put together so that it was really a thing of beauty. The artist had taken the junk and destruction of a society we all have to live with just as Aldo Tambolleni had, but perhaps with less anger, with more sensitivity, and given it form. He was trying to declare the eternal possibilities of life. The hope that men really can live. And that is the church's business. We proclaim it in statements of faith and we proclaim it in our common worship, but most of all we proclaim it in our common life, in the way we feel and think and act in this moment. If in some sense I can be a parson for the Lower East Side, and if the church is made up of people who are themselves struggling with their humanity, reflecting the tensions and miseries and hopes around us, then we can testify to the possibilities of the human spirit and human society. Certainly that is what the eucharist is about, a way of acting out the hopes we hold in common, and that is why it needs so much revamping, because right now for most of us Christian worship is a deadening and not an enlivening experience at all.

Dietrich Bonhoeffer's whole point of view can be summed up, John Maquarrie of Union Seminary tells me, with the words "To love is to let men be." That is a great sentence with a double meaning. To love means to leave men alone, to get off their backs. Think of how many brutal acts are committed in the name of love, how many stifling moments justified as love, how many mothers who sit on their kids' heads and say, "I love you," when the kid really needs to be left alone to work out his own problems. But the other side of the meaning is to create situations in which men can be. Many a man cannot be because of where he is, because of the trap he is in, and the prison walls around him.

I remember an interview I had once with the local police captain, one of the captains who did not last very long among us. I had gone to see him about a play street we were running on a Puerto Rican block east of us. Before the play street the traffic was heavy, but once the signs went up limiting traffic, it was even worse. Cars were coming both ways on the one-way street and it was more dangerous for children than before, and the police were doing nothing. When I walked in, he held out his hand to me warmly and said, "Father, it's great to see you, it's always great to talk to a priest, because we got so much in common. You and me and every man on the force had to make the same decision, whether to be a priest or a cop. Right, Father?" And I trembled inside, because I hated to think he might be right, though now I know he was. Then I told him my problem, but he never really understood, because he began a diatribe about the Puerto Ricans and their filthy ways. And there was really nothing I could say. So I finally got up to go, and then he said, "Father, it's been great talking to you, and it's great knowing of the fine work you're doing. Because if it wasn't for you and all the other clergy of this community working with those people, we'd have to go out and conquer them." And I left knowing that he had told the truth. He had told me who I was meant to be and who he was. We were both there to keep the natives quiet, to keep them from acting up. And I was a spokesman for a repressive force. Just like Switzerland, where a town with a resident pastor gets no resident gendarme. It hardly needs both. One will do the job perfectly well.

I remember another time when the local yellow journal began a crusade against a girlie show that had just opened on 14th Street. The paper is published by a gentleman who was recently convicted of income-tax evasion, but nonetheless he is the guardian of our morals and manufactures black crime waves and the like for frightened residents of the middle-class development just north of this community. The crusade began with the announcement that the local clergy were all with him in this valiant effort to clean up our community. But he had never asked me, and all I could do was write him and tell him, "You do not have my support, not on this issue, not when there are really serious problems destroying our people."

Karl Marx, of course, understood this long ago, understood that the church exists to keep the natives quiet, to maintain the social fabric. He called religion the "opiate of the masses" and he was right. Because this society and every society has a state religion whose very function it is to sustain the state, to maintain the state's order. But that is not the gospel, not to me in any case. It is not my job to fight birth control so that women will stay pregnant and off the barricades. Nor is it my job to keep men unemployed and useless and demeaned so that they cannot stand for their freedom and their rights as children of God. That cannot be our job. Our job is to let men be human, to get off their backs and create the kinds of situations in which they can be free. Why else the incarnation, why else a Lord who took human flesh but to say that the destiny of man and his freedom is my concern, whatever yours may be? It is the tragedy of Christianity that through the ages we have been concerned with something other than what God proclaims himself to care about. We look out into space, to a God out there, removed and disassociated, and then we avoid the world around us and its problems. But one of the most beautiful moments in the New Testament follows the ascension. Jesus has left the disciples and they stand looking into the heavens, as we still do much too often. The angel comes to them and says, "Men of Galilee, why stand there looking up into the sky? This Jesus who has been taken away from you up to heaven, will come in the same way as you have seen him go." He will be among us living out our lives and we his, somehow sharing with each other and with the life of the creator who made us. And God will go on being concerned with us as he was when he clothed Adam and Eve as they left Eden. When the church gets into social action or the arts or whatever, it is to let men be, to let them grow and blossom and flourish, and if need be create the situations where that can happen.

I am proud of the fact that we have never gone out looking for people to make programs or to enjoy them. We never started out to have a theatre or to create jazz concerts or what have you. We tried rather to respond to the demands made upon us, and to do so as best we could. Of course, that is difficult, because we rarely know what we want or need, yet the call comes through sometimes, and we have to be ready to hear it.

One of the deep influences on me before coming to the Lower East Side was an old book by Tom Allen, a Scots Presbyterian minister in Glasgow who wrote a book about ten years in his parish and called it *The Face of My Parish*. The first week he was there, Tom Allen looked out over the miserable little congregation in the midst of a great, empty church, and he thought of all the people outside who should be there singing praises to the Lord. So he got together a whole bunch of college students and they went out door to door, calling the people to the wedding feast. And they came, an amazing number of people who had never darkened the door of a church, or had long since forgotten when they had, and one Sunday the church was full. But the original congregation did not want them. This was their church, their sanctuary, their escape from the bitter and angry streets around, and one old lady, sitting in the pew she had long believed was hers and where she had sat alone for decades, drove out the invaders, and the Sunday after, the church was back to its same miserable little group of the dead. Then he decided that he could never again invite a living soul into that church until he had opened it up, until he had created a place that wanted to be alive and that wanted to welcome in the halt and the lame and the blind.

When I came to St. Mark's it was very closed in—not that my predecessor had failed to work for an open and loving place. And in many ways he had succeeded, but still it was closed in. Some of the people knew it and some did not. But those who did had demanded a young minister, a man free enough and young enough to experiment and help open up the church. So my job was to free the church, to make it a place where men could be, starting with the people who were there, so that they could in turn welcome in others. It took four years before anybody knocked on the door, before anybody from outside asked for anything. Four years of trying to say quietly, We want to be the church for this parish, we want to respond, speak to us.

In the summer of 1963 I got the call. A fellow priest from downtown called and asked me to go to Baltimore with him and get arrested. He told me that two hundred people from the Lower East Side were responding to a call from Baltimore CORE to liberate an amusement park that had long been a symbol of segregation and injustice. Two hundred frightened, rejected and hurt people from this community were going to serve their brothers and sisters in Baltimore. They were going to get busted and go to jail in order to be free, and they wanted their priests with them. I procrastinated. In fact the three of us who finally went played a kind of game of I'll go if you go, and then we all decided to go. Because we knew that if we did not go, we could never be parsons of this community. An old priest, a beautiful saint of a man, said to me later, "But of course, Michael, a priest must go wherever his people go." If we did not go, we would be a church in some other time, some other place, but not for this parish, nor these people. So in fear and trembling I told the congregation one Sunday that I was going, I was going to celebrate the Fourth of July by getting arrested in Gwyn Oaks Park, Baltimore. And I said I hoped I would not have to go alone. And I did not. A black woman whose divorced husband was a Black Muslim went with me because she had to tell her children that Christians also believed in freedom. A young white woman and a white man went with me because they too believed in freedom. A beautiful black man who later became our senior warden came up to me and said, "Michael, you know I don't want to go South." And I said, "I know that, Harry." And he said, "You know that I don't want to get arrested." And I said I knew that, too. And then he said, "But, Michael, you can't go alone." And he went along, I guess, to protect me, because he loved me, this man who was ten years older than I with five kids, and a job as a foreman in a garment-industry plant.

We all went together and when we got busted and were being arraigned, the cops looked at Harry with his gray hair and his quiet dignity, and said, "Hey, Pop, aren't you a little old for this kid stuff?" If only it were kid stuff and freedom were already won.

When we came back, we discovered that we were alive and the church was ready to be alive. We had a parish meeting, a very stormy one, to decide how we felt about what had happened. And the congregation finally voted to support our actions and commend us and encourage us to get arrested again in our own community. And we did. Later that month nine clergymen and a social worker from this community and one from the Diocese of New York tried to close down the construction of a housing project in the Lower East Side. It was being built to house blacks and Puerto Ricans, but in violation of federal, state and city law the City of New York was building this project with all-white labor, with the hands of men who did not live in this community, who had no stake in it, and who would never live in it. They would return to the suburbs and an all-white neighborhood out there, away from the brutalities which are everyday existence for us here.

We believed that the mayor should be in jail for breaking the law, and since he would not go, and since no court then constituted would send him to jail, we decided to go in his place to proclaim the incongruity of a law that is only unevenly enforced if enforced at all, that allows city officials to break laws with impunity, but jails the clergy and the people who demand law and order and justice.

Out of that we were able to form the Lower East Side Civil Rights Committee and with the full backing of the congregation use church space, let the church in fact be a rallying point for the school boycotts that came about that winter. The first strong demands for decent schools in the black ghettos of New York.

We did not run the Civil Rights Committee, nor did we tell the people what to do or where to go, but we did try to make possible a coalition for dignity on the Lower East Side, a possibility for blacks and whites and browns to work together for a common purpose—the freedom and dignity of every man here.

But the establishment killed us off, and killed us off hard. It was partly our fault. In the spring of 1964 our local congressman was up for reelection, and in this rotten borough which is as thoroughly a one-party district as any place in the South, the only thing that counted was the primary. Bill Haddad, a good and honest reformer, was running. But we failed to understand that the Reform Democrats were a key part of our coalition, and we went right on in civil rights action rather than hard political organization. I think we could have got him nominated and then elected. And if we had, we would have controlled the Democratic machine. But as it was, we did not understand. We simply did not know that the establishment was afraid of our voting power, our potential control over all those black and Puerto Rican and white-liberal votes. We could have turned the old machine out. But we failed, and they turned us out instead.

That summer the principals of the Lower East Side schools charged Mobilization for Youth with underhanded practices, with disturbing the peace of the community, and Senator Marchi of the state Senate accused MFY of being riddled with communists. And that did it. MFY fired some of its best men. The Lower East Side Neighborhoods Association fired our staff worker and cut off our funds, and we were crippled. The whole community was crippled, because MFY never again mounted the kind of community-action programs that were beginning to change our people and give them hope. The Young Adult Action Group had proved that junkies and delinquents can be turned into social action, and healed in the process. They had turned out disciplined groups of kids to picket schools, to march in demonstrations, to work on rent strikes. And those kids were off junk. They were out of trouble, except that deep trouble which comes from standing up for your rights. But they were cut off. The mothers' group had worked in the schools and brought the diffident and scared parents in and helped them to speak up. And when they spoke up, they demanded that disdainful, incompetent principals be removed, that books be issued to all their children—that lousy schools improve. They were disbanded. So we went back to hurting, to fearing, and therefore hating. And the nation wonders why the ghettos riot, when our every attempt to organize, to work for justice is cut off and defeated, sometimes with massive force.

I know how much we are all involved in the stifling of the human spirit, out of fear I suppose, the fear that freedom for another man means slavery for me. And that is only so because we have long made it so, and based the freedom of the few on the slavery of the many. But as I understand the Christian faith, it is the Holy Spirit's work to blow like a great wind fanning the latent flames in men's hearts, to make them act, to make them believe, to make them live out the fullness of their humanity. And therefore to change all this which kills and destroys men's dignity. So the Holy Spirit has to be hated and detested by the oppressor and sometimes most of all by a church which has too much invested in the status quo. But why try to read the Bible, or go to church, unless it is because we want to learn to recognize the voice of the Holy Spirit, so we can tell him apart from other spirits? So many voices speak to us, and they say so many things, and most of the voices speak for our destruction and our death. Adam and Eve had trouble telling one voice from another. They could not tell that the serpent's voice was leading them to destruction, and we have all had the same difficulty ever since. But maybe the principal way to tell the voices apart is to listen carefully for the voice that speaks of freedom, that denies oppression, that allows men to love and care for each other.

There are many kinds of freedom, and the same voice that called us into the civil rights movement, that demanded we be one with the people working for freedom, also called us into the arts. Because about the same time my friend called and asked me to go to Baltimore with him, Aldo Tambolleni came along and asked if he could put together a little art show. We said he could and it turned out to be enormous and vital and magnificent and it propelled us into the world of the arts.

We produced two weeks of almost around-the-clock presentations, an art show in the parish hall, two floors of the very best painting and sculpture this community could produce, jazz concerts in the church yard. And they were great concerts. I remember one distinguished jazz musician coming up to me after the concert was over with tears in his eyes and thanking me for letting him play in the open air of

a church yard instead of the smoke-filled rooms of the cab-
arets and before people who came in free and were not pay-
ing to line someone else's pocket. We showed films, the best
of the current underground films, and we thought we would
have a hundred people or so at each performance—we only
planned two performances on two Friday nights. But a thousand people showed up for the first show and we kept on
screening the films almost all night because no one had had
a chance to see good underground films in an open and free
place. Poets read and dancers danced and the seeds were
planted for many future events. Because we had said loud
and clear to the community around us, We are open to you.
Come and ask.

The filmmakers did. The police had just arrested the makers
of *Flaming Creatures*. I never saw the movie and do not know
whether it was good or bad. But I do know the police and
the legal establishment had driven a whole group of creative
filmmakers underground by their attempts at censorship. That
is why a whole generation of filmmakers are known as "underground filmmakers," because almost literally they had to
work underground. The only way a creative new filmmaker
could show his work was to find a dark basement some place
and run it like a speakeasy and act like a frightened animal
to show his film. So a delegation of filmmakers came to us
and asked for help. We got together our lawyers and looked
up New York State law. The problem was that an unlicensed
film could not be publicly screened, and obviously the Board
of Regents was not going to license any of this so-called pornography. But we also discovered that educational institutions could show unlicensed films, and it was about time the
church became an educational institution. We agreed, therefore, to let the filmmakers show films on Sunday nights in the
parish hall. And for a year close to two hundred filmmakers

gathered every Sunday night in freedom and peace to show each other their films and therefore to live, because an artist has to be produced, and he needs the criticism of his peers. Some of the stuff was unbelievably bad. You have no idea what kind of pornography we showed in our parish hall. But some of it was magnificently beautiful, and I exulted that we allowed filmmakers to confront each other and deal with each other. The best criticism of a bad film comes from a good filmmaker, and a rich process of community interaction was strengthened that year. Filmmakers were able to operate and function as human beings without harassment, without anybody busting them. The police would come around once in a while and we would tell them we did not need their services and they would leave. Then suddenly it was all over. Because the Supreme Court ended pre-censorship in New York. The filmmakers were free now to move out and show their films wherever they wanted, and whole new groups emerged, and shortly thereafter our film program ended. As it needed to. Because the program had never been for us, but for the filmmakers. And when it was no longer useful to the filmmakers, it had to end. So it must be with all the programs we mount. They last only as long as they are needed. Just as man was not made for the Sabbath but the Sabbath for man, so men are not made for programs, but programs for men.

One Sunday a man came to church who had been in the theatre. He had acted and directed, but the whole world had come apart for him. He was depressed and confused and hurt, and now he cannot remember why he came to church. But he came, and that day I preached one of my more depressing sermons. I guess I was going through some kind of crisis of my own, and that reached him. Apparently he saw me as someone in as much trouble as he was, and he wanted to help. So we went out to have a beer together and we talked all afternoon and a relationship began which became very precious to both of us. Then he began tentatively to come back into the theatre. I had muttered around for years about doing Hemingway's "Today Is Friday" as the sermon one Sunday in church. Nobody had ever picked me up on it, but Ralph heard me and began to gather together some people from the congregation to put it on. One day he announced that he was ready, and we presented it to the vestry—and lost a vestryman. This vestryman was deeply offended and declared that it would only go on over his dead body. We tried to reason with him, tried to show him that this was an act of love, but he insisted that it could not go on, or at least the dirty words would have to be removed. If he could edit the play and remove what was offensive to him, he would agree to let it go on. I tried to tell him that nobody edits Hemingway, that this is a form of blasphemy, too. So we lost him, and that was a sorrow, because he had been a fine and eloquent Christian who had helped strengthen the church in tough moments. I learned something painful out of this, that sometimes love for one man or group means hurting another, and those are the moments when hard choices get made. We had to make a choice. We could agree with the vestryman and then we would hurt Ralph and the people who had worked so hard on the play, or we could side with the play and lose the vestryman. The only way I knew how to make the decision was to ask myself which of these men could find a ministry somewhere else. And I knew the answer. There were many churches around where the vestryman could find a spiritual home, but no place else for Ralph, and we could not risk turning him away, because that meant sending him back into the wilderness and death.

Then some kids in the parish asked Ralph to start an acting

workshop, and out of it came Theatre Genesis, a theatre for beginning, where playwrights and actors and directors could find themselves and find their art. Because theatre, like the church, demands a community, and a place, in order to exist. Now new demands are coming upon us and sometimes it gets very rough. But we will survive if we really are the church in the community. If we really are the church, then we will not be the enemy, we will not be another corrupt institution that needs to be destroyed for men to be free. We will be the mirror image of every group making demands upon us, and then we can work together.

But this leaves us all anxiety-ridden, because suddenly we discover how interdependent we all are. We discover that if we are going to respond to our community and find our life here, we are going to have to wait for the Holy Spirit to speak to us and we are going to have to learn to hear him very clearly. And that means the real risk of dying as a church, even as people. Because we could be very wrong. We could be deluding ourselves at any moment. In any case, we live in the midst of a dying community and a dying nation. And the Christian's only response is to listen for the faint murmurings, the gentle sighings, and sometimes the powerful wind of the Holy Spirit offering life.

7

The church was packed. Hundreds of people filled the pews and overflowed into the aisles. Someone was talking and the people were listening intently. He was talking about freedom, and the people wanted to hear, they wanted desperately to hear about freedom and taste its sweetness and joy. And then we walked in. Somebody saw us and the signal somehow got passed along, and suddenly the whole congregation began to sing, "Glory, glory, hallelujah—his truth is marching on." I thought the rafters were going to come down. The building itself seemed to be shaking, and something more alive and beautiful than anything I had ever experienced was happening. We were not talking about freedom. We were not even singing about freedom. We were living it. Men and women, black and white embraced. We cried. We laughed. We danced. In that moment we were together. We were free and we were rejoicing—rejoicing as I had never rejoiced before.

That Monday afternoon I had been in the dentist's chair getting my teeth cleaned. I had got up late and as I went uptown I read the afternoon paper—and I read about Selma. I read about state troopers, the guardians of law and order, clubbing old women, kicking children, terrorizing the black people of Selma who had organized and demonstrated for freedom, that inalienable right which we have denied to so many men, women and children in our nation. It hurt to read this; it hurt to know that behind all our facades and behind all the values I had been taught as a child and which mattered to me was this truth. I thought of my great-great-grandfather who had graduated from West Point in 1834. He was an extraordinary man, according to family tradition. He had founded two military academies, taught mathematics at Transylvania College in Lexington, Kentucky, helped organize the postal service in San Francisco and, according to Kentucky tradition, invented the typewriter. But he had commanded the 19th Texas Infantry in the Civil War. He had fought to perpetuate slavery, to deny freedom to fellowmen, to treat human beings as animals!

I wanted so desperately to take my stand, to say as loud and clear as I could that the America I believed in was a land of freedom to be defended against the narrow prejudices and the bigotries that lurk in all our souls. But Selma was way down South and out of my territory. And I could not go unless I was called. And the call came. While I sat in the dentist's chair, my wife called to say that our national church offices had sent out the message—Go to Selma, respond to their plight. And before I could answer, my wife told me my children had packed my bag, and she had made reservations for Birmingham. So I went, and it was the church in Selma which sang out its freedom, which proclaimed that every man, woman and child there was free in his heart, free in his mind, and ready to free his captors, ready to proclaim freedom to the white men coming down from the North, and to the white men who surrounded the church with their police barricades, their malice, and their hatred.

The singing went on long enough to wrench something loose inside of me, to tell me that never again could I turn the church into a place of mourning, a place where the dead go to be confirmed in their death. Worship, liturgy has to do with proclaiming life in the midst of death, love in the midst of hate, hope in the midst of despair.

A friend of mine was chaplain of a school for disturbed and delinquent kids, and he had gone to great pains to make his ministry there relevant. He had taken one look at the dark and dreary and musty old church which he had to use, and decided it had to go. It had to be new and cheerful and light. So he had painted the church white. He had hung it with colorful banners, and he had pulled the altar away from the wall. No longer could the priest turn his back on the people, face a wall and call out to a distant and absent God. Now he faced the people and across a table proclaimed a God present and involved with his family.

But a little boy came up to him after the job was done, looked around for a long time and asked, "Father, why have you made the church look like a courtroom?"

Suddenly it was all clear. The altar rail was the bar of justice. The altar was the judge's table, and behind it stood the priest acting as judge, looking down on the people below and passing out judgment. Lord knows, the little boy knew enough about that. He was only in that school because a court had sent him there. He knew what it was to stand before the bar of justice and be condemned, judged for being a troubled child in a troubled city, destroying as everything in the city taught him to destroy. And here to be faced with it again?

Of course the child was right. The church does look like a courtroom. It was meant to be one from the beginning. Churches were patterned on the court—the great courts of Europe where kings and queens presided over their people and gave judgment, sometimes lovingly, more often harshly and with condemnation. At least it must have felt like condemnation to be a peasant and see all the glory that others had but you could never touch. All my friend was doing was bringing the image up to date, bringing it home and making it unmistakable. Think of that image, think of what it is like to stand before the judge knowing that he holds your life and destiny in his hands. He can cripple you with years in prison and name you forever a criminal—or he can free you and let you return to the society of your fellowmen to live out your life. Is God the eternal judge who passes out sentence on his guilty people? Is that what worship is really about?

Certainly if our job is to keep the natives quiet, if our task is somehow interchangeable with that of the police, then that is the God we proclaim.

A few years ago I took my wife and children to East Germany. I wanted to see what an Iron Curtain country really was like, and I wanted my children to cut past all fantasy, pro and con, and see East Germany for themselves. When we got to the border it was like entering an enormous prison. We drove down a narrow strip of road with concrete walls on either side and border guards with tommy guns walking along the top. Ahead was a plaza surrounded with barbed wire and with cars being inspected. I went into the offices and found the people cordial enough—mostly, I think, because we were not passing through on the way to West Berlin but were planning to spend ten days in their country. A Volkspolizie took my passport and my visa application form and began to examine me. He did so with mild contempt, scanning me from head to toe to get an impression of this casually attired American. And then suddenly he snapped to and, staring at my visa application and then at me, said, "You are minister?" And I said, "Yes," remembering that the form asked my occupation and I had written in "Minister."

He said, "What kind of minister?" I thought he did not understand English very well, so I tried to make him understand, and I said, "I am a Protestant pastor." He looked at me for a while and then relaxed and with mild contempt said, "Kirchen?" And I said, "Yes, church."

It took a while to understand what had happened. He had mistaken me for a real minister, for a minister of state. In my own thoughts when I suddenly saw the truth, he had mistaken me for the American Minister of Police, for somebody who really mattered—for somebody who maintained law and order and decency. And I realized that I was going to have to make the choice of being cop or priest, just as the 9th Precinct captain had told me, just as this East German policeman was telling me, and I was going to have to go on making that decision and asking myself what it meant to be a priest and not a cop. And I wondered if the contempt he had for me was really matched by many Americans who also know the truth—that a priest is just a flunky for the state.

The confusion about our role and the role of the church, however, is not limited to East German cops and delinquent boys. A few years ago I spent the day at a local seminary, talking to students and teaching a class in pastoral theology. I had nothing very much in mind. Certainly I had prepared no talk. But the dialogue began almost immediately and off we went. It was a splendid session. We talked about visions and hopes and together we were becoming prophetic and like the prophets of old telling the truth in love. But that night I preached in the chapel and most of the same students were there—formally attired, lined up in neat rows in boxed-in pews, and every one as boxed in emotionally as they were physically. I had prepared a sermon, a good sermon, and I tried to preach it. But I could not. I could not get through the impenetrable gloom, the heaviness of that chapel and the condemned men waiting for judgment. And I knew the little boy was right. The church is a courtroom to proclaim judgment.

But it does not have to be. It must not be, and if it were, I would never have come into the church at all. In fact the great religious experience for me was of a courtroom, but a very different courtroom. It happened when I first visited Chartres Cathedral. I had read Henry Adams' *Mont St. Michel and Chartres,* so I was ready. It was my birthday and my wife and I were students in Paris. We had decided to go to Chartres and spend a day and night there and see if Henry Adams was right.

We approached the cathedral through the little narrow, winding streets, and in the gray of an October afternoon we saw its great brooding facade before us. Gray, heavy limestone, a fortress, and before us massive wooden doors flanked by statues of kings and queens of France. We went in, and suddenly it was no longer gray. It was soft and delicate and warm, with a little hint of soft blue in the light. We both felt very quiet and very close, and the longer we spent there, the closer we felt.

We walked down the main aisle, into the crossing, and looked up at the rose window. But there was no window.

Instead there was the pitch black sky, and in the sky, jewels—emeralds, sapphires, rubies—as I had never seen them before, a shining radiance that spoke of all the glory man can ever know. For the stone surrounding the glass was lost in the dimness of the afternoon, and the sun shining through the window made everything else invisible. I had never seen such glory before, such vivid color, such warmth. And I did what I wanted most of all to do, hugged my wife and held her and felt like a child of God, close to paradise.

Henry Adams had said just this. He had described the inside of Chartres as the palace of Our Lady, the courtroom of the Queen of Heaven, a place of feminine radiance and warmth, a place of protection and love. And that is exactly what it was, this incredible monument to the hopes and joys and needs of medieval men erecting a statement of what matters in life, creating a place of refuge from the winding streets and the evil that brooded there—as it broods now in the streets of New York.

After a while we went outside and looked at the exterior again, and the more we looked at it, the more a whole other feeling began to emerge. The exterior is indeed a great and mighty fortress, in all its gray, massive splendor. But the more I looked at it, the more my mind's eye began to create, not a fortress, but a great stallion, nervous and tense in his muscled strength. And on the stallion, a knight with two great lances, ready to protect the palace of Our Lady.

Many years later, when we drove once again to Chartres, the impression was even stronger. Chartres sits in the middle of a plain, a little farm town to which the produce of miles around comes, and within her walls every kind of treachery and pain has existed for as long as anyone can remember. But rising up out of the midst of the town stands the great cathedral with its twin spires, the great stallion with its knight and his lances, proclaiming something precious needing protection.

I thought about knights in armor. I thought about masculinity and strength, and war and violence. All of it means nothing, worse than nothing, it is a kind of blasphemy if that armor and strength is not there to protect the precious, the warm, the feminine and the gentle. What knight ever rode into battle except there was a lady's scarf on his arm, and what lady ever stayed home except to wait for her knight, and make love on his return? Certainly that is what Chartres is about. And all French cathedrals in fact. Because every one of them is Notre Dame of something, of some town, of some place that needs a lady, and needs a fortress to protect a lady.

The church has always been designed as a courtroom, but if it is Chartres, it is not the court of judgment, but a court of freedom. It is the place where a man goes to hear that he is a child of God, made in his image, made to know his God and in that knowledge live out his freedom, his freedom to be human and warm, tender and loving.

There is an old church in Italy—the oldest left—which has only the great mosaic above the altar left standing. And the mosaic shows the Christ sitting on his throne in splendor. Above him is the dove and above the dove, the great sunburst of divinity, Father, Son, and Holy Spirit, reigning over humanity. Around the Christ sit the twelve disciples, and below, all of humanity, hands reaching up in joy, singing hallelujah and giving thanks to the great monarch who has declared their freedom, who has welcomed them into his kingdom of joy. And in front of the mosaic once stood a throne for the bishop, and around his throne chairs for the elders, and before them, the people, all singing hallelujah on earth for the promise of the kingdom of heaven, yet to come, but partially here. At least here for a moment, long enough to let us know what life can be. And this is what worship is meant to be—the proclamation of our hopes, the anticipation of what is to come, which gives us the courage and the strength to work for a new world and never to accept the old as permanent, never to accept anything less than Chartres as a model for life.

The eucharist, then, has to be a very special kind of moment—not separate from all other moments, but the summation of the possibilities inherent in every other moment. After all, Chartres was built by human hands and proclaims the possibility that the town of Chartres can produce more than groceries, more than treachery, greed, more than evil. It can produce this monument of the human spirit. If that moment were unrelated to all other moments, then it would be almost as bad as going into court for judgment and condemnation, because every moment of joy in the church would proclaim the absence of joy elsewhere and the hopelessness of the human condition.

If indeed men live between the ages, caught between the age of which Adam is the symbol—Adam the rebel and the outcast, living in the betrayal he has wrought and for which he pays the price in distrust and guilt—and the age of Christ, the age of man's freedom and nobility, then we need moments which tell us the age of Christ is here—at least in part. We need moments that point to hope, that are in some way redemptive.

Psychiatrists talk about the traumatic moment, the terrible moment the patient remembers when all his life was warped and destroyed. Every man has buried somewhere in his semiconscious mind the memory of betrayal and distrust, a memory that darkens everything he does and leads him to live as if that trauma were the final truth of existence. But the moment is only a moment—one remembered because it points to many others, the accumulation of the sadness of childhood and adolescence. Is it not possible to reverse that and talk of the redemptive moment, one to be acted out again and again which points to a whole galaxy of experience that says that life can be lived in hope and need not be only trauma?

Seminary offered that to me. We worshiped together in the morning and in the evening, but at first I held myself off, apart, in my own distrust of love and my fellow students. I was so jealous of my own individuality in all its shakiness that I could not share it, nor share another man's, and that made me alone. But gradually I participated more and more. I began to sing and respond, and I began to look into my brothers' eyes. We sat across from each other in the choir stalls, and there I could see my classmates and look at them in their varying moods and feel myself in relation to them. And what I felt there in the chapel carried over into class and into social relationships. Not right away. There was a kind of time lag, so that what I felt in chapel one month, I felt all the time six months later—which means I was growing, growing into some other experience of life led by the vision of promise inherent in the worship.

I remember the first time I recognized the meaning of the empty hands stretched out to receive Holy Communion. I knew why my hands were empty. I knew the void I felt inside of me, the emptiness of staying aloof and pretending I needed no love. But it had never really occurred to me that other men felt as I did. But one day I saw for the first time that my strongest classmates and my weakest, the smartest and the dumbest, all held out their hands empty. They were like me. But the great moments were with my wife when we knelt together with empty hands sharing the same gift of life. Then I began to see that she and I, man and woman, are not far apart, no farther apart than the artificial separations we build between us. We are really very much the same in our common human needs, our common fears and doubts and anguishes. But I needed this moment to tell me that—more, to make me experience that. Like Adam and Eve banished from the Garden of Eden, we approached the altar heavily clothed, hiding from our God, and hiding from each other. But there before the altar, where we uncovered ourselves before God, we also uncovered ourselves before each other and recognized the same humanity. And we loved.

This is a very special truth, not always found in the church, more often than not buried deliberately. At the church where I was a curate for two years, I tried to suggest the joy of worship, only to have one young woman tell me she had gone up to the altar rail for communion, and as she walked down to her pew she had smiled at her brothers and sisters, because in that moment at least they were brothers and sisters. But one dignified member had looked at her sternly and said, "We do not smile in this church." And indeed we did not. We cut people out. We preserved a little corner of respectability against the natives outside beating at the doors. And we wondered why visitors came one Sunday and never came back. We had built a mausoleum and we wanted it that way.

That is why all of us have been so concerned about liturgical reform, because somehow this moment cannot be allowed to remain in the hands of death at all, but returned to life, and to a people who need moments of shared life and hope. But honest moments when we can share our sorrows and hurts, our disillusionments and defeats, and in their midst find victory.

I am sure this is the basis of the eucharist. It is all tied up with what we mean by death and resurrection. It has to do with two lonely, beaten men on a road to Emmaus, a little village outside of Jerusalem. Their leader is dead. It is the third day after the Romans crucified him, and their world has no more hope, no more victory, only death and defeat. They meet a stranger who asks them why they are so gloomy and they ask him why he does not know what has happened— and they tell him of their friend, the man they had hoped would save his people. But the stranger starts to tell them why the crucifixion was necessary, why they had to face defeat and then learn of victory, why no man can live in constant fear of death, in constant guilt before the threat of judgment. He tells them of what it means to be dead and then come to life, and later they remember that their hearts began to burn within them.

He comes to a crossroad and looks as if he is going to leave them. They ask him to stay. But behind that asking is a decision. Do they want him to stay? Do they want to go on with a conversation that is pulling them out of their defeat and that will soon force them to work out the responsibility of being alive? The real decision is whether they want to stay, whether they want to listen, whether they want to exist in this moment and take the consequences of the moment. They ask him to stay, and in that asking they offer themselves to the moment, and the moment becomes theirs. No moment is ours, we are never really present, until we make that decision. Martin Buber writes about the moment that addresses itself to us. But we live surrounded by walls, by the impenetrability of our isolation, until we decide that the moment is addressed to us and we are ready to hear. And then we become alive. We become feeling, warm people, taking in life and growing and moving with it.

Together they walk into an inn and there they will feed their guest. But he feeds them. He has been feeding them all the time, and so it must be now. They need to take his pres-

ence into their being. They need to take the very moment
of their existence into their being—and how much more
deeply do we take it than into our stomachs and the very
stuff of our bodily humanity?

The stranger takes bread and lifts it up to God and gives
thanks for it, putting bread and life and all material things
into perspective, reminding them, and us, that this world and
our own lives are the gift of the creator. They are not ours,
not possessions that belong to us but matter held in trust for
our common good. If you do not know this, if you do not
know where your bread comes from and where your neighbor comes from, you do not know where you come from,
and you are lost and wandering on a dismal planet. But the
stranger sets it all right. He puts his life and theirs into perspective and he gives them their bread, and in that moment
they recognize their risen Lord.

They recognize him because they are doing all over again
what they have done before. Think of what happened between Jesus of Nazareth and his friends, the moments that
made them stick with him and follow him. Think of the long,
weary and troubled days, the days when they were in conflict
with their enemies, with impenetrable ignorance and malice.
Think of their days among the suffering, among the rejects
of a society that even then knew how to dismember human
beings and rob them of their dignity and worth. It is a very
wearing and tearing thing to be involved with human suffering, to know that you share that suffering, but you also helped
cause it. In the final sense it builds you up to heal and forgive
and love, but it also tears you down and drains you. I can
imagine at the end of the day the disciples, weary and down-
hearted, reclining somewhere by the side of the road or in
the house of a friend, and Jesus feeding them, giving them
their bread and wine, and talking to them. Talking to them

about what had happened during the day, trying to make sense out of it, giving them solace and comfort, and restoring their humanity and dignity to them before they went to sleep. And this was happening again. In this moment at Emmaus, breaking bread with the stranger, they knew he was there. They recognized him because they were men again, with hope, and joy, and strength.

The day we were all arrested for blocking a building site on the Lower East Side, we went to jail. We were locked up in the 7th Precinct, and a grimy place that was. Upstairs above the squad room and the desk was a little corridor with cells— little tiny cells, each barely big enough for one man. The walls were of steel plate, and the steel-mesh doors looked out onto a blank wall. The cells were side by side, and we were locked up in a long row, next to each other but unable to see each other, and very much alone. I looked around my cell. There was a bare board as a cot—a toilet with no seat and no toilet paper, and a bare bulb glaring in my eyes. The thrill was over. The excitement had gone, and now I was alone and facing the consequences of my act of civil disobedience. Each of us was very quiet for a while, each of us sinking into his own gloom. It was sunny outside and we could hear the traffic, but we knew now what it was like to be locked away from friends and family and made into a metal man imprisoned in steel, separate from flesh and blood.

Dave Romig, the minister of a Presbyterian church downtown, suddenly boomed out in his enormous voice, "Shall we praise the Lord?" And he asked if any of the Episcopalians had a prayer book. I did and so did Bill Dwyer from St. Christopher's Chapel and we were at opposite ends of the cell block. We began to read morning prayer and we all boomed out the responses. We sang hymns. None of us knew more than a verse of anything, but we knew enough hymns so we could make a loud and boisterous noise to the Lord. And our spirits began to soar. Because once again we were free men, free men in jail, beyond the reach of man's slavery. I led us in prayers and prayed for the city, for freedom, for the police that they might act justly and walk humbly with their God. But we never quite finished. The police came and took us away—to get our prayers and hymns out of the cell block, to get the taint and color of freedom away from those walls. But we had celebrated life in the midst of death, freedom in the midst of captivity, and we had tested the faith. We all know now it can stand far more serious tests than that. But we had to learn.

Five thousand Roman slaves wanted to march on Jerusalem and throw the conqueror out. And they wanted Jesus to lead them. They were prepared to die rather than live as slaves. And later their children did march on Jerusalem and they did die. The city, the country, everything they knew went with them, and Israel perished as a nation for two thousand years. Still this seemed better than slavery. But not to Jesus, who knew the tragedy of action born in despair and not hope, who wanted to promise life and freedom, not death and destruction. But words are sometimes empty, and only when we find symbols that speak more deeply than words can we sometimes communicate at all.

Jesus told them to sit down, and he took bread from a child and held it up in the air as if to say, Watch me now. I am going to act out something for you. He gave thanks for the bread and proclaimed this moment and this place a feast, a great banquet of five loaves of bread and two little fishes. But the people knew what he was doing. They knew that to break bread together is to make a common pledge. To share life is to pledge life. Jesus was pledging himself to them, and they to him.

He broke the bread and distributed it and they ate as much as they could eat. How they did that I have not the slightest idea. Maybe they all broke out their own lunches and shared, and that would have been good, because then they would have been pledging themselves to each other as well.

When it was all over, Jesus sent his friends out with twelve baskets to pick up everything that was left. Twelve baskets for the twelve tribes of Israel. Bread which men have shared and which they have identified with themselves, and themselves with it—and all the bread picked up and put into the twelve baskets. Is not human life as valuable as bread? And if all the bread is picked up and put into twelve baskets, will not Jesus pick up all those people and put them back into their tribes, and into a free people, a rebirth of the time when the twelve tribes of Israel lived in peace and justice and freedom? "Gather up the fragments that remain, that nothing may be lost." He proclaims the value of every fragment of humanity, the incompleteness of a world, a society in which some men are lost and forgotten.

But the people misunderstand and cannot accept the pledge and act out their lives in the confidence of the creator's promise to them. So they try to take him by force. But he disappears, as he must whenever men try to take him by force, whenever they try to manipulate history, or each other. But he has made them a promise, a promise to be with them in this life, walking with them, hurting with them, finally gathering them up into a new world of freedom and justice. But the promise depends on their willingness to see him in the moment, to see him all tied up with simple things and simple moments. Because the promise at the Last Supper that the bread will be his body and the wine his blood is a promise to be revealed in the ordinary moments of life, in every moment, and never apart from existence as it is and will be.

Martin Buber tells a lovely and enigmatic story out of the Hasidic community of Eastern Europe. It is about the Baal Shem, the master of the holy name and founder of the Hasidim. A young rabbi goes to see him, and asks him to teach him the mystery of life, because this the master of the holy name must know. And the Baal Shem says, "Yes, my son, I will, but on one condition, that you ask for no more." And the young rabbi agrees. So they walk out of the house and into the Baal Shem's carriage and start off down a dusty and dreary road in a dreary countryside, and the Baal Shem begins to talk about the mystery of life. And as the Baal Shem talks, the young rabbi begins to feel the carriage mount, and suddenly the carriage is soaring. They are above the world, and he looks down and sees the world the way God sees it, and seeing it as God sees it, it is no longer dreary; he sees its incredible beauty, its hidden patterns and mysterious colors. Suddenly he hears the birds sing and behind their song he hears the very music of the universe. He gets more and more excited as discovery follows discovery and he takes in all the magnificent beauty of creation. In ecstasy he turns to the Baal Shem and says, "More, let me have more." And they are back on a dreary country road and the Baal Shem says, "My son, you ask too much."

Somewhere in there is something about our own life, and about our own worship, about accepting the gift that is before us, about accepting a God who comes in the obvious and the common—as well as the beautiful and sublime.

Martin Luther, whose great contribution to Christianity was to make it earthy and vulgar and common so that we might all the more see its incredible beauty, said of the Mass something like this, "Be well assured that when you go to the altar you shall receive the body and blood of our Lord Jesus Christ. If you go in faith, you will receive it alive, life unto life. But if you go in disbelief, you will receive the body and blood of our Lord Jesus Christ as a rotten, stinking corpse, death unto death." Luther went on to say that so it is with life. If you receive your neighbor in disbelief you will receive him dead, and every human encounter will become more painful, because each will remind you that you and he and everyone you know will die. Then life becomes a series of separations and losses, rejections and hurts. But in faith every human encounter promises increasing life, more encounters, greater love. There are yet more beautiful moments ahead. There is love you know nothing about, which the Lord will send if you will but wait and accept this moment as the prelude to the next.

Luther said that Christ is present "in, with, by, under, and through" the Mass, as he is present in, with, by, under, and through all the moments of life. Never to be equated with the moment, with the Mass, with anything, not even to be equated with the man Jesus of Nazareth who was God's own hidden revelation of himself, revealing only as much as he chooses to reveal. We live in the context of mystery, and if we do not, we do not live in the truth but in some small lie which is convenient, but cold and dead as a faithless world is cold and dead.

The poet knows that the greatest truth cannot be stated directly, cannot be rationalized and packaged for logical consumption, but that in the poem, in the moment, in the person, the truth is shining through for those who are prepared to accept it as it is offered. And I think the eucharist is a moment like that. A moment in which we uncover Christ, in which we see revealed before us the Christ who was always there, but we did not know him, or perhaps want him.

If in some way we are all parsons, men and women working out our identity in this time and this place, then the eucharist is the supreme moment when we do that, when we try to put together a community of promise and hope in which we can act out the truth we believe to be basic to life, that men were created for freedom and joy. That is why we call our Sunday service at St. Mark's the "parish eucharist," because in some sense we are doing something for and with the parish when we gather together. We are part of the parish around us and we bring the parish in with us when we come.

One Sunday the church was packed, our church in the middle of the Lower East Side, and it was packed with the strange and sad people who make up the community. Lots of young people dressed in wild and colorful costumes, middle-aged artists and intellectuals, blacks and whites, freaks and straight people, and here and there Puerto Rican children and Slavic teenagers, a mix that could never mix. I stood at the door in my eucharistic vestments, in those strange old robes that priests still wear and which take on a special kind of relevance where everybody else is wearing antique clothes. I knew what was there. I knew how many pot heads and speed freaks were there. I knew how much perversion and lust men and women had brought with them. Somewhere there was a man who had sold his soul to the police and was an informer, the man who appears at every rally, every demonstration, and some church services to tell the police what plots we are cooking up. And up in front was the Mind Garage, a bunch of college dropouts from the University of West Virginia, kids who wanted to make religion joyous and beautiful, who wanted to play rock music to the glory of the Lord.

It certainly was a strange group—but it was the parish and that is where we begin. The drummer, black and beautiful, clad in a dashiki, silhouetted against our timber cross, began to beat on his cymbal, a sharp ringing of the bell—the call to worship. And on the drum a heavy beat, beginning, swelling. And we all said, "We are here—we are here in the name of Jesus Christ." We who have no name and no place, who belong to an angry and bitter community, surrounded by an even angrier community—we are here to find a name and find a place and time to be. And the ministers walked down the aisle as we said who we were and acknowledged what we had brought with us—evil and despair. And suddenly a roll of the drums and the rock music began, crashing, screaming, shouting with exuberance, "Lord, have mercy; Christ, have mercy; Lord, have mercy." We rejoice that we can come here, that we can stand before a Lord of freedom and love, who will make us people and give us a moment we cannot have by ourselves.

The drums quieted. The music slowed, and we read the lessons, the reminder that we stand in history, that we have a past, that God has always been working with his people, always calling them out of cities and caves and jails and palaces to new life, new hope, new visions. Then I preached. I remember that it was a very simple statement about a drummer, this drummer whose father died yesterday, who went home yesterday to bury him, but is with us today because he has to live, as we all have to live, and not get caught in death—who wants to offer us his music, and we can offer him our love.

We sang the creed, with a wild beat and electric guitars, not as if the creed were a test to pass, a series of dreary doctrines to learn and disbelieve, but as the marching song of Christians, as the affirmation that we believe in someone beyond ourselves who will lead us and restore us.

We prayed. No one led the prayers. We just stood quietly, and as each person knew what he wanted to pray about, he did. Some of the prayers were lovely and tender, some were bitter and angry. A few were selfish and proud. But nobody said we were good people in this church. Just men, just the Lower East Side trying to find itself.

We made peace, not finally, not forever, because some of us would fight later and some of us would leave in bitterness one day, but we offered it in anticipation of another day, a greater day when all men could live in peace.

And we offered what we had to give. Money. Dollar bills rolled off the presses to pay for Vietnam, to build segregated swimming pools, to maintain rotten ghetto schools, to bribe building inspectors and cops, to pay for dope, money that represents our lives and our sweat, good and bad, but us. We offered bread, wheat grown by farmers who eke out a bare existence, or grown by robber barons who exploit the land and the people with their machines and their greed. Bread baked by underpaid workmen, filled with rotten chemicals. Bread that is eaten in greed, stored away to rot if no one has the price to pay.

We offered wine, and outside the doors of the church winos lay in the sidewalk drunk from bottles of cheap muscatel—briefly escaped from their terrors and fears. Wine that comes from crushing grapes, spilling the juice and letting it ferment. All these mixed and ambiguous products of human society, offered on the table of the Lord asking that he accept them, that he accept us, that he make us free of them, free of our captivities, and then through us proclaim to the whole parish what it means to be a child of God.

We blessed the bread and the wine—that is, we offered them up to the Lord and asked him to use them and us for a new life. As the Lord did it once in Jerusalem, in Emmaus, wherever men have been weary and disillusioned and needed strength and hope, so do it now, Lord, feed us, and go on feeding us until the new world comes. We broke the bread and distributed it, and every man fed his neighbor and was fed by him—as it must be in the new day when starvation and greed are gone, when war is gone and men live in peace and love.

The music began again, and the people began to dance. All over the church the people were dancing. A group of young men picked me up and heaved me in the air as if to offer me up—and to teach me to trust in their hands and their love. And all the while we danced, we did so before a great wooden cross we had made out of tenement floor beams. It was big enough to use, big enough to nail a man on and rob him of life, as those beams had robbed men of decent life and decent housing all the years they held together a rotten tenement. And it reminded us, as the very service reminded us, that we always dance before a cross; there can be no other kind of dance in a world made up of crosses. So we cannot take the dance lightly. We cannot forget the cross. Our lives are too precious for that. The moment is too fleeting. And then we left to tell the parish what had happened to it through us. We had offered it in all its evil on the table of the Lord, and he had accepted it and given it back to us, renewed, another day to start again, to make a new world. That is the eucharist for me.

8

One of the very best of the young American playwrights was talking to me. He began with Theatre Genesis and now has written a movie, been produced at Lincoln Center and will be heard from more and more. He was telling me about some of his problems, and we had talked a long time when he said, "Mike, I think St. Mark's is doing great work. You're out in the community. You're working for the people." And I waited for the "but," the "but" that follows many a compliment. It came. "But how about meditation? What have you got to say about meditation? The Swami down the street is packing in the kids and he tells them how to meditate. The Beatles have gone to India to find out. What about you?"

I thought about that. I thought about our poor, sad church, Christians out of contact with the terrible tensions and pressures of this country, battling for lost and dreary causes, giving their all in crusades against smut, and ignoring poverty and war. And how infinitely sad that this playwright believes we have very little to say about meditation either. So what is left that we do know about, that we do care about?

Of course it may be that we know very little about prayer, because we know very little about social involvement. It may be that in fact they are related enough so that you cannot do the one without doing the other. If you do nothing at all, then you have nothing to pray about. And if you go long enough without prayer, you may find you have nothing to do, because you see nothing and feel nothing. I suspect prayer has to do with finding out where you are and what is really going on around you. It cannot be some other kind of living, any more than the eucharist is something else you do, some other compartment of life which is relegated to Sundays and the back sections of *Newsweek.* Prayer has to do with this moment, with seeing it and knowing it.

Paul talks about seeing no man from a human point of view any longer. As if we could see men from another perspective, from God's point of view. As if there were greater depths to life than the obvious and the immediately offered. The greatest sermon of them all, the basis of all preaching, is Peter's, on the day of Pentecost, when the disciples found new life and new hope and danced in the streets, proclaiming this joy. "You think they are drunk," said Peter. "But let me tell you the truth. These men are caught up in the Holy Spirit. New life has begun for them. Can you not see that?" But perhaps we cannot unless we find new eyes and new ears, unless we have a way of seeing and hearing that greater truth which is God's point of view.

Thoreau has a beautiful image of the man who marches to the cadence of a distant drum. But how do you hear the distant drum? How do you hear what your fellowmen do not hear? Of course part of the answer is in the common worship of the church. Part of it is in music, poetry, theatre, in those moments of extraordinary clarity in which other men have seen and known the truth and are willing to share it. But finally there has to be a moment when a man hears and knows the truth all by himself.

I remember in seminary working out a kind of practical understanding of what sin and forgiveness mean. Day after day I went to chapel, and day after day I looked across at the faces of my friends. If I could look them in the eye, if I could smile and feel myself one with them, then I knew I was forgiven. But if I could not, if I hid my face, averted my eyes, if my classmates looked at me with anger, then something was wrong, with me or with them, and something had to be repaired. And I was sure Jesus' admonition to the disciples to forgive sin—and to judge sin—was wrapped up in the community of common worship. So I told the dean of my discovery and he nodded, then said, "But, Michael, there will be moments when you will stand absolutely alone, when you will stand against the community, and when you must find the courage to believe you are right, and they are wrong." A man must make a moment to find himself, and to do so alone.

A priest in a neighboring parish preached a sermon about St. Mark's—a sermon denouncing us for our heathen practices and our impiousness. I knew about it through a friend and I was proud, because I would have been deeply distressed if this particular priest had commended me. After all, men are known as much by their enemies as by their friends, and it is a terrible sadness to be liked by men you hoped would find enough truth in you so they would have to denounce you. My friend told me the priest had read an article about St. Mark's in the Sunday *Herald Tribune*. I think it was called, "Is God Dead at St. Mark's in the Bowery?" And it was full of the scandalous things we were doing—theatre, poetry, jazz. The priest was furious and, standing in his pulpit shaking the article at his people, said, "The church is for worship. Not for this!" But my friend told me he was preaching to a tired and dispirited group of people, nodding in their pews, oblivious to the world around them, to the priest and, I suspect, to themselves. And it occurred to me that he knew as little about worship as I did. Before that young playwright he was as lost as I.

He did not understand that it was the hard-core gut-level worship of this congregation that had driven me out into the community to get arrested, to picket, to battle for human rights. And it was the same worship that kept me from more fear than I could handle, that kept me from cowering in a corner when the going got rough. It was the worship that made possible the theatre, the poetry, the unusual things we had done, possible because we were not afraid to try and risk failure or criticism, because something kept coming alive in us and moving us into action. But the opposite was also true, that the thing we did, the action we took, the risks we ran made the worship vital and real and strong, too.

I went through clinical training in seminary. The first summer was at Boston State (Mental) Hospital, the second at Boston Psychopathic, where I was part of two separate and consecutive groups of seminarians involved in a difficult and shattering kind of experience. We were becoming part of the hospital, sharing life with patients and staff, living in an indeterminate world, partly staff, partly patients ourselves. And three times a week at Boston State, every day at Boston Psycho we would meet for group dynamics—for hard encounter with each other. Each group began the same way, with a kind of mock love. After all, we were seminarians, all

Christians together in a common experience. But very quickly the layers began to peel away. Our fears appeared, and our anger, and we began to tear each other apart. That was deeply frightening to men unwilling to admit their anger and fear, to Christians taught always to love. Then we passed through that anger to another level, a whole new experience of love and understanding. At least we did at Boston State, and in the last group at Boston Psycho. We did that, I think, because each of us was heavily involved in the life of the hospital, involved with patients, sharing their sorrows and their anger. And each day when we came into our own group, we brought the hospital with us, and we asked each other for help in coping with our burdens. This is what kept us alive: the group supporting what we each did in the hospital, the hospital forcing the group to love or perish.

But it was different when we began at Boston Psycho. We moved quickly into rage—and stayed there. We chewed and gnawed at each other and no love ever happened. No new day ever dawned. We were too concerned with ourselves. We did not care about the hospital. We had decided to concentrate on our little group, to figure out its dynamics. So we fed on each other. Having nothing to bring into the group, we took nothing out. And we slowly starved ourselves, until all we could do was chew each other up and use each other as food.

St. Paul struggled with this question. He knew that where men risk life, where they risk frightening evil, they also find truth. He said that where sin abounds, grace the more abounds. Where men live and suffer and sin, where the need for forgiveness is great, so will be the forgiveness. And he wondered then if a man should go out and sin in order to be forgiven. Martin Luther struggled with the same issue— and his confessor even more. There was a time when the confessor, weary of hearing Luther's interminable confessions about trivia, urged him to go out and commit some crime, something serious enough to demand the kind of forgiveness Luther yearned for. Both finally rejected the idea that we should sin in order to be forgiven, but both demanded that we live, that we run the risk of sin in order that we might build and not destroy or decay. So Luther speaks of sinning boldly, by which he means living boldly and running the risk in the knowledge that the Lord will forgive.

Clearly men with no problems have nothing to solve and no need for faith or hope or forgiveness. Like the man I called on when I was a curate. His little girl had just started Sunday school with us, and I made the necessary call. His wife announced that the child was in Sunday school in order to learn Episcopal manners, which surely was the truth, but I was amazed that she would be so honest. Most of us are not. Then he told me how religion was necessary for troubled men like myself, but clearly unnecessary for successful men like him. I asked him if he had been in World War II. He had. He had been a Navy flier—an ensign. I told him I had been a second lieutenant in the Engineers. Every once in a while I wondered what it would be like to be back in the Army. I thought of going back as a second lieutenant, and I knew that was easy. I had already done that. I thought of what it might be like to be a captain, and I decided I had enough general experience to do that. But what if I went back as a colonel? For that I would have to go to church a lot and pray a lot to have the courage and the stamina to make it. "The difference between the two of us," I told him, "is that I am a colonel now and you are still an ensign."

I guess that was arrogant, but there was some truth in it. Certainly my concerns were far deeper now than they ever had been. That very spring I had stood by a teenager who had lost her father, and the next week by a wife whose invalid husband had died in surgery—breaking apart what was left of her life. And the next week the most beloved teacher in the church school had died on the operating table. And when I went to the hospital to see her husband, he glared at me and said, "Dammit, don't tell me this was God's will." And then the next week the beautiful old priest I worked for died, as suddenly and unexpectedly as the others. And that meant I was in charge of a parish that had broken better men than I, and which in many ways had broken the old priest. It had taken a great deal of support, a great deal of love, a great deal of profound worship to get me through that spring.

But the level of a man's concerns are really the measure of his maturity. It would be tragic to be concerned about the same things one year that had mattered ten years before. It would mean that nothing had changed inside, nothing had grown and developed. It would be like a man and wife looking at each other and knowing that their love was the same now as it had been when they were married years before. It would be the admission of some kind of spiritual death.

Life has some similarity to that old New England rock farmer plowing up rocks year after year. Every year he hopes that there will be no more rocks—but finally clear, soft soil. And there never is: just more rocks, but always deeper and harder to get out. If a man is not plowing up those rocks in himself, he probably is not growing.

Prayer has something to do with finding the rocks, with deepening concerns. It has to do with finding one's own soul and making contact with the inner man. It has to do with finding in that inner man the evidence of something beyond, of some deeper level of experience coming to us always, but rarely enough recognized. Certainly the hallucinogenic drugs have revealed whole levels of experience we rarely recognize. A doctor I know has researched LSD and claims to have found whole levels of sensory awareness we have never recognized. I would rather do the same thing through meditation and prayer—but I know I would be a poor man indeed if I did not find some way to know the depths of myself and of the world around me.

At a party once I met a doctor doing research on dreams. He was not a psychiatrist but a physiologist, and he was not concerned with the content of the dreams, just the dreaming itself. He had discovered, he told me, that men must dream in order to function, that every human being dreams forty-five minutes a night plus or minus a minute. There is no necessity for sleep, though there is a physiological need for rest. And it happens that we all rest best when we stretch out flat on something soft—and inevitably we go to sleep. But that is not the real issue. The fact is that you have to dream forty-five minutes a night or you come apart at the seams. He did some research on this and discovered that if he put an electroencephalograph on a man's head, his brain waves changed whenever he dreamed. So he hooked the EEG up on the heads of all those poor loyal people who show up for experiments like this and woke the subject up every time he began to dream. The first night he could wake the subject up four or five times and keep him from dreaming. The second night it took twenty or thirty times to keep him from dreaming—and the third night they were at it all night long. The man was frantically trying to dream and keep himself together. Because if they succeeded, after the third night the subject started to come apart. He walked around in a daze and he could not coordinate his movements. So dreaming, the doctor said, is basically essential to your physiological existence. And then he looked me in the eye and said, "Father, what do you think about prayer? Are there any possibilities that prayer is a form of dreaming, daydreaming perhaps, which makes it possible for you to function on a whole other level of your existence?"

There is no research on that. Certainly no physiological research, and very little psychological or spiritual research. There are some men who pray a lot and are obviously better men for it—and some who are not. Some of those families who pray together may indeed stay together—but they may also poison the atmosphere with their smugness.

But it is at least an interesting possibility that something may need to grow inside of you, something of which you are only dimly aware, but which is the difference between being fully human and not—the difference between seeing from God's point of view and not.

I know that the fifteen years or so I have been a Christian have been hard years—much harder years than any I knew before. I have faced more misery and despair in myself and around me than I ever did before. They have been painful years—but they have also been beautiful years, and in the midst of all that was hurtful I have also found beauties I never knew existed. Now I think I understand something that Dean Taylor said to me when he was leaving the seminary for another ministry. I told him how much he had meant to me over the two and a half years I had known him. And that was true. This beautiful man had led me into depths of experience and knowledge I had never before touched. He had taught me the faith. He blushed a bit when I told him what he meant to me, and then pulling himself up tall, he said, "Michael, don't lean on a broken reed," and walked away. He had a far greater sense of his own unworthiness than I did of mine. But he also had a far greater sense of his own dignity and grandeur as a human being. He had experienced more of himself than I ever shall unless I can reach the level of his humanity. And

that experience of oneself and of the world is an experience
of life and death, misery and grandeur.

Sometimes I wonder if prayer is not a little like creation
itself. If we really believe that creation is somehow continu-
ous, that the Lord is always at work pulling order out of chaos,
mercy out of contempt, love out of hate, victory out of defeat, he is also pulling me out of choas, and always forming
me as a man. If you accept the lovely Hebrew notion that at
night God loses his grip on creation and lets it fall back into
the edge of chaos, then we also slip into the primeval every
night. And every day we have to come back and in some manner be re-created. Certainly this is true of me. Many a morning comes as a great shock. I am not sure I am yet awake. I am
not sure whether the dream has ended and the day begun or
not. And I know I need to be pulled back into form and
meaning and purpose—and this means laying myself open to
the Lord so he can do the work, so he can call me all over
again. If you also consider the possibility that you and I are
Adam, who was drawn up out of the primeval stuff and
formed into a man, with the breath of God blown into him to
make him alive, then the breath of God has to come to me if
I am going to live fully—at the level for which I was created.

It has always seemed to me that if the Christ is the full revelation of God—and of the image in which we are made—
then that image is revealed in a cohesive, integral, functioning
person. And the opposite—the devil—must precisely not be
personality, must be disorder and confusion and personal
disintegration. Certainly there are demonic forces constantly
at work to dismember us all—both physically with the ex-
plosives that blow a man's body apart, and mentally with the
lies and fantasies and waves of hate that blow a man's mind to
pieces.

The New Testament talks beautifully of the man whose

name was legion—who was a whole succession of people, all of them in conflict. So he was never together, never one man—until he met Jesus, until he met a personality so strong, so real, so full that it forced him together in response. And the end of the matter is two men in dialogue, two men open to each other and able to walk together or apart through the rest of their lives.

So prayer must somehow be me letting myself fall under the influence of the great personality, of the source of personality, and becoming a man in the process—an ever larger man as I grow into the fullness of the stature of the one to whom I relate. But there are some problems about this. Because if you really are going to pray, then you are going to come under the influence of someone, something greater than yourself and be dominated by him. That is very frightening, except that in a curious way unless you allow yourself to be dominated and overcome, you can never be free. Remember the great image of the knight who only becomes a knight and only becomes free as he kneels before the Lord and swears obedience. And the greatest knights were those who served the greatest masters—"whose service is perfect freedom," says the prayer book.

I knew a professor once who studied with one of the great theologians of our time. The theologian loved his student. He was the apple of his eye, and he believed that his student would someday be a great thinker, the great theologian of his own time. But it never happened and never will, because the professor is still at work fighting off his teacher, still criticizing, still pushing away, still afraid of being dominated. The disciple can never move beyond the master he does not accept and love.

There is a curious little passage in Paul's first letter to the Corinthians about the human personality. Paul says, "Among men, who knows what a man is but the man's own spirit within him?" If my spirit alone knows me, then only as my spirit goes out to you and is in you, can you know me. And that is very frightening. Does it mean that we only know others as they dominate us? But if you do not take that risk, if you do not accept a man's spirit in you, you will never know him. You cannot relate to people at a distance without touching them, if not physically, then spiritually and emotionally. And this must be true with God.

I know that my own first prayers as a Christian were deeply terrifying. I knew what Francis Thompson was trying to say in *The Hound of Heaven*. I knelt down to pray and it was as if an ominous presence were approaching, preparing to envelop me and dominate me. It was terrifying. It was a little like the desperate fear of the girl in Bergman's *Through a Glass Darkly*. She felt God, she knew him as a great spider, as an object of terror, as destroying presence, coming to take her away into eternal horror. To her, then, the encounter with God was ultimate disaster—and in the end she dies a spiritual death. And this I feared, too. But it never came. Instead, the more I prayed and the more the presence enveloped me, the more I knew that God was not a spider God, that this presence was coming to love me and not hate me. It was as if some demon inside of me were crying out to the Lord of creation, Go away, leave me alone, let me live in this man and delude him and blind him. Certainly this is what the New Testament records, the terrible fear as Jesus approaches, but the fear of the demon within the man, the presence of evil—the primeval chaos inside of me resisting creation, resisting order and meaning.

Prayer is therefore always a struggle and always difficult. When I was first a curate, I used to try to kneel down in the church and meditate. But the temptation was strong, desperately strong to be up and about, to be doing things—mindless things, acts unthought on. And only the very greatest self-discipline kept me there trying to decide what was really important and what I had to do that really mattered. But that is the history of Israel—the people who struggled with God, who struggled with him because they also know evil and struggle with it. And the goal is to find the truth, to find the direction.

I remember when I was in seminary my best friend accused me of some dark and desperate betrayal. I did not know what it was about. But I was angry. I was angry at this friend who had rejected me. And I went to the chapel to try to work it out. I knelt down and my prayer came out in a mass of feeling. I pleaded with God to avenge me, to destroy my friend. And I thought of all the ways the God of Israel, the Lord of the armies, who visits the sins of the fathers on the children, could do this thing. I savored my own anger, and then it began to taste bad. And the anger began to subside. Something else was welling up inside me. And the something else was hurt, my own desperate hurt that my friend had rejected me, that I had lost someone I loved. And then I wept and asked the Lord to give me back my friend. That is what prayer is about for me, finding out what I really feel, what is really happening, and listening in the deepening quiet of my own soul for the truth.

Adam stood before God with a little fig leaf and tried to hide. And what a silly moment that was, the creature hiding from the creator—Adam hiding from the one "unto whom all hearts are open, all desires known and from whom no secrets are hid." He was not hiding from God—only from himself. So I am not sure that prayer has to do with telling God what we want and where we are. I suspect he knows already. But it has to do with telling myself the truth the Lord already knows, admitting to myself where I am and what I have to do. It is really coming to terms with myself. Just as Adam finally had to confess that he was hiding, and then he could talk to the Lord, and, more important, the Lord could talk to him. And Adam in his new honesty could hear the Lord's honesty. But until then, we play a game and everything else remains suspended. The truth remains hidden until we stop. Karl Barth, with some deep sense of man's self-delusion, calls this age in which we live the "age of God's patience." The age in which God in his patience waits for man to be honest with himself, to accept the bounty that is here, if only we will see it and admit it.

Because I feel this deeply, I have always loved the Eighty-first Psalm, the psalm which speaks of God's suffering—the Lord who gave so much to Israel and Israel refused it. It ends with these lines:

> Oh that my people would heed me, that Israel
>   would walk in my ways!
>
> At once I would subdue their foes, turn my hand
>   against their enemies.
>
> The Lord's enemies would cringe at their feet
>   and their subjection would last forever.
>
> But Israel I would feed with finest wheat
>   and fill them with honey from the rock.

If only you had come to me—but you did not want me. Adam has to take that miserable fig leaf off. He has to stop hiding and admit the truth to himself. And that is why we pray. Not to tell God anything, because he knows it already, but to tell ourselves the truth, so we can hear the Lord.

In moments of desperate anxiety, when the problem is too big and I know I cannot handle it, then I kneel down and I try to keep quiet. And that itself is the battle, to quiet me inside, to quiet the voices shouting within my head, the demands, the fears, the doubts. And if finally I can quiet down, then other voices begin, other thoughts and feelings emerge, and I can be a man; I can do what I have to do.

Thus it was with Martin Luther, who stood before the Diet of Worms and defied all the power there was in Germany. It was as if he were standing before the Supreme Court, the Senate, and all the university presidents of this land, saying to them, "I cannot. I will not recant. By God's grace I can do no other. Here I stand. Amen." It took enormous courage, enormous belief to do this, to defy the church and the state, and stand alone.

But the courage of the afternoon came from the prayer and tenderness of the morning. That morning Luther had knelt by the bedside of a dying young knight. Tenderly, compassionately, he prayed and wept and consoled, and helped a frightened young man face death. Only when the knight died and when the prayers were finished would Luther leave. So the soldiers assigned to escort him to the Diet stood outside the room and waited—and took him away to meet his fate, a tender, gentle man who out of that quiet roared like a lion. I suspect that the man who cannot do what Luther did in the morning, cannot do what he did in the afternoon. Maybe it was as if each man were a kind of Chartres Cathedral, with the strength to fight if he must, to stand fast if that is what truth requires, but gentle and warm and loving because otherwise life has no meaning.

When I was in seminary, no matter when I went to chapel, the dean was always there before me, his head in his hands, deep in prayer. At first this puzzled me, because no one was stronger or more powerful than Dean Taylor. He was the most austere Yankee I had ever known—looking and behaving as if he were chipped out of Vermont granite—a very beautiful man to those who cared enough to find him out. But there he was, his head in his hands, kneeling before his God, admitting his inabilities and his needs and his wants, crying out perhaps for support in meeting the daily demands of life. And then I began to understand, to know where this man's strength came from, and I began to unbend and open myself and admit my needs. Perhaps a man can only really be a man, strong, vibrant and alive, when he is willing to be a lamb—like the lamb of God who was often a lion.

Ignatius Loyola once said a curious thing about prayer—something very contrary to American religion. He said, "When you pray, pray as if everything depended on you. When you work, work as if everything depended on God." No American would say that. Because we know that prayer depends on God and work on us. Once a week we check in, burden the Lord with all the problems we cannot or will not solve—like praying for peace or civil rights. Then we go off and fight the war and wreck the society and leave the Lord way, way out of our lives. But Ignatius is saying quietly and gently that no man palms off his troubles on anyone else. Yours they are and yours they will remain. Neither does a man forget the Lord of history—except at his own peril. He cannot act as if the world belonged to him and as if he could do what he wanted. In the final analysis the truth will be served—or man perishes.

Primitive people knew this better than we do, and they ritualized their knowledge and danced to be one with their God and what he was doing. So the Navajos danced before the rain, not to make it rain—they were not concerned with magic—but so that when it did rain, it would be good for them and make their crops grow. They wanted to share in the rain, to share in what God was doing. And in a sense then they were being obedient to the will of God, to the will of nature. This is what Ignatius means by working as if everything depended on God—working in rhythm with the Lord of creation who is always ordering and creating his universe.

One of my favorite characters in the history of Christianity is Bernard of Clairvaux, certainly one of the strangest of saints. He spent six months of every year tearing Europe apart. He toppled a pope, started a Crusade, destroyed Abelard, and made it very clear it was he who was the real power in Europe. And then suddenly he would disappear and return to his monastery, the most austere and ascetic of all the monks. There he slept on the floor, used a log for a pillow and practiced all the most severe self-inflicted deprivations and tortures of the medieval ascetic. Only to emerge again six months later and dominate Europe. He was certainly one of the most in and out characters we have produced in this society. He was in fact the classic mystic personality. The man of prayer and action, the man of extremes. It was as if he had to reflect deeply on what he had done and what he was going to do. He had to communicate with God and leave himself, leave the world, and tune in on the deepest part of himself to find what he had to do in the world. And then he acted, strongly, fiercely, creatively.

I am not sure you and I have to go through the six-month cycles—that could be pretty rough on our employers and families. But perhaps we need to go through something like this every day. Maybe every day the Lord re-creates you and pulls you back into life and tells you what it is he wants you to do this day. So I have always prayed in the morning with my date book opened, asking what I shall do and whom I shall see. If I do not ask for some kind of guidance from those inner resources where I think the Lord sometimes speaks, I am making a fundamental mockery of my religion. I become like all those Christians who say that the faith has to do with spiritual matters—and the worldly matters of life and death, hunger and pain, belong to someone else.

The dean of my seminary said once about prayer, "Before you do anything at all, pray about it. And if you cannot pray about it, don't do it. And after you have done anything, give thanks to Almighty God for it, and if you cannot, don't ever do it again." This is a pretty hard point of view, but Puritans are hard, and perhaps a world as hard as ours demands something more than sentiment from us. Could a man pray to the God of the New Testament and in obedience to that prayer use cattle prods on small black children? Could a man honestly give thanks to the God of creation for a day spent pumping stinking chemicals into a river and further destroying our common planet? If he could, then he lives some kind of profound lie and perhaps ought to be honest about that.

To pray before you do anything, and to give thanks for what you have done, implies beginnings and endings in the midst of the ongoing current of life. It implies that you and I make decisions about our lives, and therefore to some extent at least are free men, free to choose what we shall do. But what, then, are the beginnings? Sometimes I wonder when my own day begins—or my week, my month or my year. Does my day begin when I roll out of bed? Or when I have my first cup of coffee? Or does it begin when I make conscious decisions about what I will do today and therefore enter the day awake and alive and ready to live? I am sure this is a problem for many of us who find that whole days, weeks, months have passed without our stopping to consider what we have done, to savor the quality of our own lives, and to make something important out of ourselves. How frightening to consider that

I might not know what day it is or what time it is—or who I am, because I never stopped to ask or consider, but let life drift away senselessly.

I know it matters to me to go to church once a week, if only to say one week is over, another has begun. And sometimes I try to think what this week has been about, and I try to think of what the next will mean. St. Paul talks about redeeming the time—about making it mean something. And I am sure he means being conscious of the time and conscious of me and what I am doing.

Maybe because my own chaos gets very deep indeed, prayer means waking up and beginning the day and recognizing that it is today and I am going to have to deal with this day. I am going to respond to this moment which is addressed to me. I am going to try to know what the moment is saying, so I can be one with it and move with creation. But to do this I need to silence myself. And that is a hard job because so much is happening inside. But if I wait long enough and am patient enough, in the last minute or two everything slows down and I get my directions and I know what time it is and what to do with the day.

9

We slept on the floor and it was very hard and very cold. I decided I did not like sleeping on floors. We were in the home-economics room of Junior High School 271, which means there was a lot of peanut butter and jelly around to eat during the night. It had never occurred to me that home economics depended so heavily on peanut butter and jelly, but in New York apparently it does, because there were vast quantities around the room. That was good, because none of us had eaten any dinner, and we did very little sleeping. I think I slept about an hour, wrapped up in an overcoat on the floor. We were all too excited to sleep. We had too much to say to each other.

We started gathering together Tuesday afternoon because Herbert Oliver, the head of the Ocean Hill–Brownsville School District Governing Board, had called us for help. A settlement of the school strike that had kept all of the city's schools closed for weeks had just been imposed on them. The strike had begun because the Ocean Hill Community Governing Board had fired a large number of union teachers— teachers who, the community claimed, were incompetent to teach their children. And Lord knows, the record of those schools indicated that something was drastically wrong. There is not a single ghetto school in New York where the reading levels are up to par. And everyone knows that the worst teachers in the system end up in the ghetto schools. Since no one can fire a union teacher, the incompetents get transferred—and eventually they all end up at the end of the line, the ghetto school. And Ocean Hill was the end of the ghetto-school line.

The governing board was willing to let the union teachers come back. They knew they had lost their fight. But they sure wished they would go away, and if you had met some of the teachers in question you would have wanted them to go away, too. But the governing board in good conscience could not accept the other demands put upon them. They could not let two black principals and one Puerto Rican principal be suspended without a hearing and with no charges against them.

The strike had been called to protect a union teacher's right to due process, and many a civil libertarian had sided with the union for that reason. It was bitterly ironic for the strike to end with the denial of that same right to nonunion teachers and principals.

So Mr. Oliver wanted our support—the support of those white clergymen who were prepared to stand with their black brothers. It mattered for us to be there, because still as clergymen we had a kind of force, a kind of symbolic position of conscience in the community. How much longer that will last I do not know. Certainly we have revealed ourselves as something more than the moral eunuchs the community once thought we were. Maybe we can still prick the conscience a bit. I hope it will last.

The three principals who were being sacrificed to the union wanted our support, too. They were among the very few black and brown principals to get past the incredible machinery built up over the years to keep out the undesirables—the blacks and the browns and the people who did not walk in step with the existing bureaucracy. Only one or two blacks and no Puerto Ricans had made it through before, and in a city as heavily black and Puerto Rican as ours that was in itself a tragedy. So we were going to join the principals in their schools and tell them they were not alone. We would spend the night, and in the morning when the police came to remove them, they would have to remove us. It is still true that the police treat middle-aged, middle-class whites better than they do blacks and browns, even if they are school principals. I guess the community smarting under its defeat wanted some of us to share in it, some of us to know how much it hurt to see a great experiment in community control of the schools destroyed. And we wanted to manifest some basic American ideals of justice.

We talk a great deal about America now. Every time I see a car go by with "Honor America" or "America, Love It or Leave It" on the bumper, something shrivels inside me, and I ask myself if my fellow citizens cannot understand that some of the rest of us love our country, too. We love it enough to want to protect its ancient liberties, and we want to correct some of its ancient injustices. We want slavery in all its forms to end once and for all. We want black people to have the same inalienable rights that other Americans have. But how do I say that on my bumper or in my car window? A good friend of mine, the junior warden of the church, made his suggestion last Christmas. He gave me an enormous American flag. The pole reaches to the ceiling and the flag is as big as I am. I guess I could wrap myself up in it. But it is not the Stars and Stripes. It is the first battle flag of the U.S. Navy—the first flag under which Americans fought for their freedom. Red and white stripes, and a great serpent in thirteen parts, and the motto, "Don't Tread on Me." That is the way I feel. That is the America I love, the country founded in the defense of liberty, the country that could proclaim government of the people, by the people, and for the people. So the flag stands beside my desk in my study—a reminder and a hope.

But we had better all find something soon, because our liberties are in serious danger. And they were in serious danger that day in Ocean Hill. We had been through a long strike to defend the rights of white teachers, and now we were going to take away the rights of black teachers, rights so recently won, so little exercised. So we slept on the floor of Junior High School 271 in Ocean Hill–Brownsville, proclaiming the rights of an American to freedom, to respect, to justice. And the very best people were there. Three Catholic priests, for example, who were almost ready to leave the Church. They were fed up with their white parishes, fed up with the Church's indifference to blacks. So the bishop had let them get an apartment in Bedford-Stuyvesant in the heart of the worst ghetto of them all, and they were trying to find a new ministry, and they were almost succeeding. They wanted to show their black brothers and sisters that they cared. There were some school parents, some seminarians, including one from St. Mark's. And in the middle of the night he and I talked about the ministry and where it has to be exercised. I guess we agreed that it had to go beyond the doors of that old church and out of the Union Seminary classroom. There were a group of Christians from Judson Church. They had all come together, and here they were proclaiming their parish's concern for another parish, another community.

But best of all was a beautiful and powerful Christian layman named Harris—the principal of JHS 271, the man we were supporting. He cared, and every move he made, every word he said revealed a man of deep conviction, of profound warmth and enormous intelligence. And I thought about some of the white principals I had dealt with on the Lower East Side, men and women who treated blacks with contempt but the Ivy League parson with respect; men and women who were time servers, escaping every night from the ghetto to their homes in the suburbs. They were not the best we had. The white community rarely gives its best to the schools—even the white schools. But Mr. Harris was the best, and I wondered if perhaps the black community cared more about its children than whites do.

Later on I met Rhody McCoy, the black administrator for Ocean Hill. He has a sign on his desk that says, "Speak the truth in love." It is not directed to others. He is not that arrogant. It is directed to him, and I think he reads it again and again every day. Because he does speak the truth in love. He sits at his desk quietly, puffing his pipe, listening and responding with gentleness and warmth. A little like St. Paul, I guess, he feels the need to repeat again and again to himself —Be patient, be understanding and loving. I know why St. Paul did that, because he felt that he was none of those things, but rather irascible and impatient. And he was obviously one of the most loving men who ever lived, or he could never have pulled so many churches together. Rhody McCoy probably doubts himself, too. But then the ones who love the most are the ones who doubt it the most.

I think he is the kind of man who could lead me into the

Promised Land. There is certainly a lot of feeling like that in Ocean Hill, the feeling that we are moving on the road to the Promised Land. There is no defensiveness, though Lord knows they are defending their very lives, their very hope. While all over the nation white people are getting ready to defend their honor, their homes, their privileges against the black militants, against the Black Panthers, against phantoms of our own imagining, and against the fears that arise out of the repression white America has maintained and encouraged these many years. Who wants to spend his life forever defending shabby little truths, petty privileges, and dubious honors? Why must we act like the pioneers locked in the stockade, holding off the Indians, when we could be marching toward the Promised Land, when we could be going together, winning each other's freedom? My ancestors went to Oregon and Kentucky out of hope, not out of fear. So our nation was built. On fear it will die.

Ocean Hill in Brooklyn is a real desert. I doubt anybody would deny that. Its problems are real. There is nothing very much to defend, there being so little to begin with. But the people there do have hope. I think some of them believe that they are on the way to the Promised Land. The Egyptians are probably on the trail, and they know the Red Sea lies ahead. But they believe they will make it. And I do, too. Because if they do not, none of us will.

In the morning the state trustee came by and told us the police would not remove us. We would have to leave, or he would close the school. And the very presence of the state trustee was an insult, this man who had been placed in authority over the district in order to keep the natives quiet, to make sure that Rhody McCoy and Herbert Oliver pulled off no freedom moves, or tried to live out their mandate to run their schools for the benefit of their people and under their control. None of us had thought he would threaten to close the school. That would be the last blow. Because the Ocean Hill schools were the only ones that had stayed fully open throughout the strike, the only ones in the city where the children came first. And JHS 271 was the symbol of community control for the whole city. Mr. Harris was on the spot. All his own allegiances were in question. Thank God he stood with the children. He agreed to leave peaceably so the school could stay open. But he demanded the right to get the school day going, to make sure there was order in the school. Not that anybody else cared. The school was supposed to have seven assistant principals to back up Mr. Harris. Five of them had quit rather than work with him and accept the community's control. One black assistant principal was being dismissed along with Mr. Harris. That left one assistant to run the school all by himself. A school that was trying to set new educational standards for ghetto schools, that was trying to prove that black kids could learn, too. And the strike settlement was putting ten union teachers back into the school, incompetents or saboteurs, men and women who hated the whole concept of community control and of black leadership. But Mr. Harris planned to go peaceably and pray that somehow the school would make it. He could not be the man who finally closed it down, who ended the noble experiment. He cared more about the children than about himself and his rights and privileges. But if you plan to lead anybody into the Promised Land, you had better care more about them than yourself.

I am not going to pretend that we were right in what we did. My lawyer and good friend promised to defend me in court if I got arrested, but made it clear that we were disrupting the schools and endangering any chance for peace in the city. And now two years later the strife goes on, and nobody knows anymore how we are going to resolve it. But then no man ever knows that he is right. Sometimes I get through a day believing that I am right in what I am doing—and then all the doubts come back again. But at least I stand in a great tradition. Oliver Wendell Holmes wrote to Harold Laski about the great failure of the American liberal. He is sensitive and aware, so much aware of every side of every issue that finally he is paralyzed and cannot act. Then Holmes said, "The true courage is for a man to stake absolutely all on a premise that may be disproved tomorrow." I think that is probably a pretty basic Christian idea. I know I have no blueprint for life and therefore no way of knowing from day to day whether I am on the right road or not. I find it all very risky and therefore I live on the edge of anxiety a lot of the time—and sometimes not even on the edge of it.

But the alternative seems to me to be to play chess with life. To make a move which I know will lead to a counter move and then my move and on into the dim future. It presupposes rules and patterns about life which I cannot believe exist. So I will not play chess with life. In fact I will not play chess at all. I cannot deal with it.

Maybe that is why I am a Christian, because I believe that the only coherence, the only pattern to life is God. And he stands above and beyond life, revealing himself in it, making his demands upon us, and waiting for us to respond. That means I have to listen carefully today and do what seems right today. Knowing that I may be wrong, knowing that I may have to reverse my course later, but prepared to take that risk, because finally I believe God forgives and will forgive my mistake and give me another chance to start again. I guess I believe that every day is a new chance, a new beginning, a new hope.

I believed Rhody McCoy and Herbert Oliver. I believed

they were speaking the truth because they had a vision of
the Promised Land, and the vision was a good one, one I want
to share. Like Martin Luther King, they dreamed of a land
where blacks would have the dignity they were created to
have, in which black children would get the same education
white kids get in Scarsdale and Beverly Farms and Palo Alto.
They dreamed of a land in which black mothers would get
health care that was the best this country could give. Their
vision was of justice and peace, of men living in love with
each other. It is the vision that drove my ancestors west It is
the same vision my grandmother remembered and repeated
to me. These men were very much like her, men raised on
the Bible, raised to believe they were the people Israel,
wandering in the desert, living off manna, led by the word
of God and on the way. "Praise God, I'm on my way," sings
one of the great spirituals. I am sure they confuse their
kids, as my grandmother confused me, and I hope they never
straighten them out, that they never stop thinking they are
the people Israel. Somebody in our midst has to believe
this, somebody has to believe it for the rest of us who have
forgotten or never knew, who have a jaundiced view of life
or, worse, live in despair.

Sometimes in fact people like this live as if they were in
the Promised Land already. They mete out justice; they
freely love, as if the great day had already come. It is very
beautiful when men do that. So I believe they are right, as
right as men ever get, and I will follow them.

It seems to me that the most important commitment a man
can ever make is to loyalty and trust between men and
women. I will do things out of loyalty to another man which
I would do for no other reason. I would rather act on that
basis than in response to some great truth or some great
ideal. I distrust them. I know the power of men to becloud

and confuse hopes and ideals, but I trust the capacity of men
to live in love, in response to God's call through men.

The women recognized the risen Lord by his voice. They
had known it before. They had known the tones he used and
the feelings he projected and the kinds of things he said. They
knew the cadences and nuances of his voice—and they knew
the kinds of things he did not say. They had seen him in many
situations and dialogues with other men and they had become accustomed to his voice. So of course they recognized
him when he spoke—and they went right on recognizing him
wherever they heard the truth spoken in love.

But of course it is very hard to recognize a voice you have
never heard. It is hard to recognize the truth if all you ever
hear is lies. It is hard to recognize somebody who is talking
about subjects you do not understand—and that is why we
go to church. I can think of no better reason. In order to get
to know that voice and to get to know the kinds of truth he
speaks. You go to church to become really familiar with that
voice so you will recognize it wherever and whenever he appears, in all those strange places the Lord frequents.

Dean Taylor said to me one day, "I wouldn't count on the
Bible doing very much for you now. But if you read it carefully and go on reading it, twenty years from now you will
be a different man." I think he is right. I know I think in different ways and hear different truths now. If you get accustomed to listening to his voice in one place, you may end up
hearing it elsewhere. Maybe that is the preacher's job, to try
to point out the voice as it speaks among all the other voices
of the world.

The Christian faith deals with the world's problems, but it
does so theologically, in terms of that strange and haunting
voice the women heard at the tomb. And it deals with the
world's problems because what other problems could we

possibly deal with? If you do not deal with the world's problems, then you are not dealing with the problems Jesus dealt
with, this man who healed men and women here and now,
who threw the moneychangers out of the temple so his
people could gather together and unite. The issue is, What
point of view have you got in looking at the world's problems? Do you see them through the eyes of *The New York
Daily News?* Or *The New York Times?* Or any of the limited
and narrow visions men have? Or, like St. Paul, are we prepared to see no man ever again from a human point of view?
If you begin to see men from God's point of view, it is as if
you had climbed a mountain. There you can see the whole
world as you have never seen it before. You can see its patterns and its destiny, and the world is never again the same.
You cannot go on pretending that everything is for the best
in the best of all possible worlds, nor can you pretend that
the world does not matter. It all becomes intensely serious
and intensely beautiful in potential and terribly ugly in actu-
ality. Once you have seen the world from a mountaintop,
you begin to see a kind of consistency in life that is above it
and through it and in it, but never to be equated with it. One
thing I do know at this point of my life, there are no simple
patterns in life, no designs in history or anything else. Only a
fool sees them, and he invents them to hang on to something
else that is not true. We always try to find patterns and struc-
tures of meaning, and they always collapse. Karl Marx probably comes the closest to having a reasonable philosophy of
history, and it makes great sense as long as you leave out the
breakers of system and patterns. As long as you leave out the
heroes and the intense villains who never fit any pattern at
all. Marx knows all about Adam, but he knows nothing of
Christ, who is forever breaking into history and destroying
our patterns and our goals, as if we were forever building

towers of Babel and the Lord were forever confusing our tongues and destroying the towers. Because the difference between the patterns of Adam and God are that the one is for the aggrandizement of some men against the rest—and God's are for the glorification of all humanity and all creation.

We try to find meaning and form where no form is. We try to find it in the earth and history itself, when the form and meaning is in the creator alone. Look at what we do to the Bible. We find consistencies and patterns in it which are simply not there. What makes the Bible fascinating are all its inconsistencies and contradictions and confusions—and its only unity is the Lord who pervades it. One of my professors suggested that the test of any good theology is to take God out of it and see what happens. Very little generally. But take God out of the Bible and nothing is left—even the language is destroyed, that strange and beautiful Biblical Hebrew in which God speaks in one tense, the tense of independent action, and man speaks in the other, the tense of dependent action.

Karl Barth got into an argument once with his contemporary and fellow theologian Emil Brunner. Brunner maintained that the Bible was not all sacred, but partly profane, and Barth, who lived on a mountaintop somewhere listening to Bach in the serious moments and Mozart in the light ones, said that the whole Bible was profane, every word of it, because it was written by profane men. Then he went on to say that the Bible is a little like a telephone conversation overheard. You can only hear one voice, and from it you must imagine the other. So the Bible is man's dialogue with God and all we hear is man's part of the conversation. In, with, by, under and through that conversation we will hear God, if we hear him at all. But it will take care and growing sensitivity to hear him and not the men alone.

There is a heartbreaking French film, *La Guerre est fini*, about an aging revolutionary, a man who fought the Spanish Civil War with all his life, passion, and conviction. But the war has been over for twenty years and he is still fighting it, and at the end of the film, he dies in Spain, for a lost and dead cause. "The war is ended," says the film's title, but he cannot give it up, because if he did, he would have nothing left, because he really cannot come to terms with the moment. So he goes on clinging to the past and never confronting the Lord of that war, who is also Lord of this moment. He does not know that every movement dies, every hope man has dies, all his causes and his goals and his dreams. Only the Lord of the moment and the Lord of the dreams survives. And the task is to know him so you can go from movement to movement, so you can know what time it is, so you can live in this moment and then for the next.

I had a very good friend, a Swedish artist, who really understood the faith in deep and profound ways. He and I used to talk far into the night. He made Kierkegaard seem simple and direct in comparison. My friend talked in wide, mystic circles and only after listening to him for an hour or two could I ever get the gist of what he said. A beautiful man, but terribly obscure. Then one day he left St. Mark's, because he had committed himself to the peace movement. And that was some years before Vietnam became the unbelievable horror it is now. I begged him not to leave the church. Not that he should deny the peace movement, far from it, but that he should also stay with us. I asked him to give his heart to peace and devote his every waking hour to the movement, but come once in a while and spend some time with us, and try to find the mountaintop and remember what it is like up there. But he could not do that. He plunged into the movement and he gave up his Lord and when the

movement failed for him, as it must always fail for everybody
sooner or later, he was naked and alone and afraid, with nowhere to go. So he wandered in the desert with no guide and
no vision of the Promised Land. And it pained me deeply, but
there was nothing to do.

Have you ever thought of all those grim ex-communists
who go around making speeches about the horror of their
own past? It is really very sad to see all these ex-believers
giving their little canned talks to frightened people. I suppose
it is because their God failed and the movement betrayed
them as every movement betrays everybody. Their God, their
cause was simply too small. Among all those books I have
never read because the title is almost too good to allow the
book to spoil is *Your God Is Too Small.* Your God is too small
and therefore you are too small.

I remember once serving as Protestant chaplain in a Jewish
hospital. There were understandably few Protestant patients
so it was not a very hard job. The supervising nurse went
around once a week and asked patients if they wanted to see
the Protestant chaplain, and every week she gave me a half
dozen names or so. One week I went in to see a man who
had asked to see me. I asked him how he was doing. He
glared at me and through clenched teeth said, "Fine." And
that was the end of the conversation. The next week he asked
to see me again and again he dismissed me with a hostile
and terse reply. Finally the third week his name was still on
the list and this time I entered his room with great wariness,
waiting to see what he would do. But now he looked pretty
good. He was sitting up in bed and I said good morning. And
he said good morning. So I tried to think of some way to
get a dialogue going and I saw some plays by Lillian Hellman
on his table, so I said, "Oh, plays by Lillian Hellman." And he
said, "Yeh, plays by Lillian Hellman!" So then I picked up a

magazine I had never seen before. I forget its name. But on its front cover was a list of articles, including one by William Z. Foster, the chairman of the American Communist party. That gave me a clue to what was going on. So I asked him what kind of magazine it was, and he said, "Socialist"—and in answer to the next question, "Marxist." Then I began to get the message, and the dialogue began. In the process he accused me of being a social democrat and God knows what else. It turned out that he was a communist who had been jailed under the Smith Act—and pretty bitter about it, which was certainly reasonable enough. And he had decided to play games with the Protestant chaplain. So we both drew our swords and somewhere in the midst of the fray I said, "It's pretty tough standing on the edge of the abyss, isn't it? It's hard to look down and see the void. Now, there are some of us who are going to go on looking into that abyss and we are going to keep our honesty and our integrity. And then there are some bastards like you who can't take it, and you've got two choices, to become a communist or become a Thomist. Either way, you build yourself a system and you don't have to look at the abyss. Well, I've got more guts than that, brother." And I walked out. It was a pretty arrogant statement and I am not sure I was telling the truth about myself. But I know I was right about him. He had to have the system and the tight boxes with all the answers. But that system is ultimately going to fail, because it is not good enough. And the pressures of life and change will become too great and then the bitterness and futility will set in.

The Bible knows all about that. It is not really monotheistic at all. It knows many, many Gods, all of whom have their little businesses. They set up their little stands here and there and attract their clientele—health Gods, love Gods, war Gods, Gods of valleys and mountains, all of them very busy, each working out his little area of life. But the Bible knows there is only one God over all the Gods, only one God of Gods and Lord of Lords, who reigns over all moments and all causes and places.

I have lived on the Lower East Side for eleven years. It has been a harrowing kind of existence. I suppose I enjoy it or I would have left long ago. I have watched the movements and the causes come and go, and the battles get won and lost, mostly lost. I have watched committees get formed and then get torn apart, and groups collapse, and new ones built. And sometimes I get very discouraged and I say to myself that I cannot start again. Not again. My own church is a kind of passing parade where people come and go. If you want built-in insecurity, stick around with a church in a flotsam and jetsam community where you never know if they have gone away mad or just gone away. Programs collapse and need rebuilding. I yearn for the fall when at last I will be able to say, "Let's do it the way we did it last year." But it never happens, because every year is different and we have to find new ways of responding to the people and their demands. Sometimes I shake my head and say, How can I be fool enough to stay here amidst all this stuff where nothing is solid and nothing is stable and everything comes and goes? But what other road would I follow and where else would I go?

Only to some other place with all its turbulence and its attempts to find life and meaning in that place at that time. And either here or there, I will keep going, because I believe I am on the way to the Promised Land. I know I am in the desert. I know it very deeply, too deeply sometimes. But I also know that I obey and serve a great Lord who will offer me the only consistency and direction I will ever have. And that I will only see that consistency as I look back and review my life. He will tell me about the future, and only when he is ready.

I remember at that same Jewish hospital a lovely old woman, black and from somewhere in the South. In the early mornings she used to sing spirituals in a very soft voice, really to herself. But the nurses told me the whole ward became silent, and everyone strained to listen to her songs of hope in that terrible desert where women were dying every day. She was dying, too. And I found that out one day when she said to me, "Reverend, I have a secret. You mustn't tell anybody. You mustn't tell the doctors or the nurses. They are very young and very frightened. I have cancer and I am going to die." I was very young, too, and very frightened. But it was hard to be frightened with her.

Then one day I saw her and she told me she was afraid, and I could see it in her eyes. Then she said, "But I have known my Lord Jesus all my life. I have lived with him and he has loved me. And just think, very soon I will see him face to face. Why should I be afraid?" The next time I went to the hospital she was dead. She was seeing the Lord face to face, and I know she was rejoicing.

I am not sure anybody has to take her words literally. I am not sure I did. But I knew her spirit, and something of her quiet hope came through to me, and it is that hope I speak about, that hope which in the midst of life we have as a support and a direction, which someday will be justified and proven—or maybe not proven at all. The final irony of Justice Holmes's great statement is that we may finally be proven wrong in God. But I would rather live this life in Christian belief and risk the disappointment at the end than never know hope and never believe I was on the way to the Promised Land.

Certainly I have known defeat and disappointment. There

was a moment when we all believed that we could win some battles. But we did not. And that moment is gone, as all moments and movements go. But the Lord remains and the community remains and the people remain. If you are going to be a Christian, you have to believe that in the midst of the problems and the tensions and the despair, the Lord will tell you what to do. He will tell you in your heart or in some external command you recognize as true or in some chance encounter.

And when he speaks, it will mean a struggle. Because often enough the Lord's voice is not soothing or calming or even believable. Sometimes it goes against the very basis of a man's life. But the people Israel knew that. Because their name means, "He who struggles with God." And that is their self-identity. Jacob, preparing to go home, preparing to meet his brother and coming to terms with his past and his future, wrestled with the angel. He wrestled all night and faced himself and his God. And then his name was changed to Isra-el, he who struggles with God (El). His greatness was not his goodness, or his rightness, but his struggle. He never forgot God, or ignored him. He disobeyed him, provoked him, but always struggled with him. And that is the history of the people themselves. Their own history is one long struggle to try to understand how they could possibly be the chosen people and suffer so much. It is terrible to recognize that for a thousand years the chosen people showed no remarkable signs of being chosen or favored. Rather they went from slavery to slavery, and all they had was their God.

In my own heart the great book of the Bible is the Book of Job, the struggle of man and God. And how badly misunderstood that book is. Archibald MacLeish, who knew what it meant to be Job, who saw his friends suffer for their righteousness, nevertheless wrote a miserable play—*JB*—making

Job a character from a Norman Rockwell *Saturday Evening
Post* cover. But Job is a great man, a giant of a man of honesty and integrity and beauty. A kind of Albert Schweitzer.
It is as if that great man were sitting in Lambaréné, his hospital burned to the ground, all his assistants and his patients
murdered, his daughter dead, and his wife loathing him, as
he sits there covered with boils. Covered with, drowned in
every human affliction. And then he calls out, "My God, why
have you done this? What have I done?"

Job poses the basic problem of injustice in God's world.
Why do good men suffer and die? Why do decent and hon-
orable men live in poverty and humiliation, while the captains of the Mafia live in regal splendor, corrupting our police
and our courts? Why did six million Jews die while the
Western nations refused them asylum and supported their
killers?

Job cries out in anger and despair, demanding to know
why a just man suffers so. And his friends come to him and
give him the very best answers that human society has been
able to find. They are so fine that the Episcopal Church uses
them sometimes for Sunday readings, answers about the
punishment of sin, about suffering producing manhood. But
that is not the issue. It does not matter whether Job's friends
are generally right or wise or not. Their answers just do not
apply to Job. And Job refuses to compromise his integrity and
honesty as a man by accepting their petty answers. Just as it
is tragic now when men buy peace of mind or soul at the cost
of their honesty and their integrity by loyalty to a system that
denies the pain, cruelty, injustice and filth that are always
found in life. They may live in relative peace and comfort—
but always at the cost of an absurd understanding of life, and
therefore at the cost of hiding from the truth, lest it spoil their
system. This is the danger of all systems and answers, that the

price is very high. We remain as little as our answers and our systems, rather than grow into the fullness I believe we have been promised. So Job demands his answers from God and God alone. He turns away from his friends. He cuts loose from his past and there he stands naked and alone before God, demanding the truth. He shakes his fist, he rages and shouts. And God shouts back. He thunders out the question, "Where were you when I created the universe? Where were you when I made man? How can you know the answers? How can you understand who I am and what I am?" God gives him no answer, because God is and remains an eternal mystery forever beyond the reach of man, revealing only what he chooses to reveal and nothing more. God hidden, forever hidden, the sign of the enormity of the universe, and revealed, the sign that he cares for us.

Finally God puts him down, shatters him and throws him to the ground where Job repents in dust and ashes. Not of asking the question, however. Not of challenging God. No man will ever discover his humanity if he cannot shake his fist at God, if he cannot shout and rage like Job. But Job repents of believing that he could ever know the answer to his question, that the universe could ever be so small that man could understand it and grasp it and control it. Job wanted to make the world and God too small. He wanted to bring God down to him—when the great mystery of life is that God will bring man to him, that God offers us an ever enlarging humanity in his ever enlarging universe. And he sends Job back to the world of suffering and pain to live in that greater knowledge which is the love of God and not answers.

It is like St. Thomas, who of all the disciples held out demanding to know whether the resurrected Lord was the same one he had known making his way among the hurt and the lost and the broken. Therefore he wanted to see the wounds, the sign of God among his people. And only then could he call out, "My Lord and my God." That is where we will find God, where he is in the world ministering to it and loving it and believing in it. He gives no answers. There are no answers except that God offers to love us and make us close to him and therefore close to life.

At a party once a man asked me with that kind of belligerency some men have about religion, "Tell me who your God is!" And the only answer I could give was this, "My God is the one who allows me to know nothing. He allows me to live without answers, and not needing them. He allows me not to settle for a little world or a little God, and he even allows me not to know who he really is. But he does allow me to be free to be a man. That is who my God is."

10

A black man in a dashiki stood in front of the cross. It is a great cross made of the floor beams of a demolished tenement in our neighborhood. Someone had stolen the silver cross given to the church as a memorial. So we had gone out into the community and stolen three gray and ugly floor beams. We knew what they meant. We knew the exploitation, the misery and the poverty and humiliation that had been lived out above and beneath them. So we had made a cross out of them, great beams bolted together with black iron bolts. And now the Black and Brown Caucus of the church had put up three banners behind the cross. A great black, green and red flag in the center. Some people thought it was the very same black liberation flag that had hung over a battleground in Harlem, a sign of black freedom and self-determination. Now it hung at St. Mark's.

On the other side of the liberation flag hung a green banner with a great black fist in the middle and above it the words, "There can be no peace without freedom." Malcolm X had said that, knowing the Old Testament far better than we do and predicting the truth of the late 1960s and the 1970s of our nation. And below his words the Swahili *"Uhuru Sasa"*— "Freedom Now." On the other side a black banner with a lightning bolt in the center and the Spanish words *"Alerta —Boricua e Hispano—illego la hora—la unión hace la fuerza —Libertad."* Also a call for freedom and liberty. The black man was guarding them. Telling the congregation by his presence who had put them there and why they were there.

The congregation sat dumbfounded and confused. They did not understand. A few months before, we had discussed James Foreman's confrontation at Riverside Church. And we had discussed the Black Manifesto. We knew it could not happen here, because this church had been deeply involved in the civil rights movement, and the blacks had always been free at St. Mark's. And now they were telling us this was not so. They were destroying our illusions about ourselves, and we were afraid and some of us were angry.

Just a month before, in July of 1969, we had appointed David Garcia to the staff as assistant minister. We knew that the church was out of touch with the black and brown communities, but especially the brown community. We were surrounded by Spanish people, but hardly a Spanish person was coming to church. And we knew this was wrong. We knew we had to be a racially and ethnically mixed congregation. We knew we had to be involved with the life of the whole community if indeed we were going to be the church in the parish. And I knew that I had to be more involved than I had been for a long time.

So we had a Chicano assistant minister just out of Colgate

Rochester–Bexley Hall Divinity School. We knew he was militant and we knew that only a militant Spanish minister could
serve the people around us. We knew he had been involved
in the Black Caucus that had closed down the divinity school
for three weeks that spring and demanded justice for blacks
in the school. But we never imagined anything would happen
to us. We expected him to operate out of St. Mark's and do
justice in the community, supporting us all the while.

But that Sunday the Black and Brown Caucus made its first
appearance, and we were in for some real confrontation. The
blacks and the browns were trying to tell us something about
ourselves, something we had not heard—that no matter how
liberal you may be, you are part of a racist system, and you
reflect that racism and act it out in everything you do.

By the time I came back from summer vacation the congregation was in real trouble. The black and brown members of
the congregation were sitting together, refusing communion
and refusing to give or receive the peace. And that hurt us all.
We had been close. We had been loving. It mattered to us
that we passed the bread and the wine through the congregation, each person there feeding his brother or sister—all of
us acting out the hope of a new world in which all men
would feed each other and no man would ever go hungry.
It mattered to us that we made peace, not as a sign of the
present, but as a sign of our hopes for the society, the hope
that men might live in peace. But all of this was threatened,
all of it under attack. I wondered what would happen if David
at the altar refused to give me the peace. What would I do?
I never found out, because he and I were never together at
the altar that month. But one black woman who had been at
St. Mark's longer than I had, whose daughters were in many
ways my daughters, whom I had known and loved for ten
years, refused to take my hand after church when I returned at

the end of that summer. And that hurt. It hurt terribly, and I
knew then that I was involved in the great crime of our nation, that nothing would ever remove that truth. God, and
my sister, might forgive. But the truth remains.

Then it happened. One Sunday in October, the whole black
and brown congregation stood up together and surrounded
our free-standing altar. John Clarke, a young man who had
grown up in the parish, who had carried the cross for me as
an acolyte, who had picketed with me at Seward Park High
School, who had tried to get arrested with me at Rutgers
Housing Project, read their manifesto. The blacks were
accusing us of plantation mentality, of racist practices, and
they were making demands, hard demands, real demands, not
symbols.

The manifesto demanded that the congregation seat three
blacks and a Puerto Rican on our vestry immediately. It demanded that the church turn over $30,000 to the caucus to
be used at its discretion. It demanded that the worship of
our parish be made relevant and meaningful to black people.
It demanded that a black and brown arts program replace
or coexist with the white arts program. And finally it demanded that I begin to serve the community through the
Black and Brown Caucus.

Each demand hurt, because each demand judged us and
found us wanting. Each demand said we had not really been
brothers and sisters. And that was hard to take.

When John Clarke finished reading, he said they were
going to leave the church, and they hoped anybody who believed in their demands would follow.

That was a hard moment. I had heard men and women
whom I loved, and who had loved me, judge me, judge us
all. And I wondered what I should do. Should I stay there and
continue the service? But I knew if I did that, no black would

ever trust me again. I would be saying that I stood with the whites. I stood against people I had lived with and loved for ten years. But if I walked out then, there were whites who would never speak to me again. There were whites I would hurt and friendships I would lose.

It seemed a long time while I stood there and wondered what my ministry was all about. What was the truth for me? And where did I stand?

I walked out. I followed the blacks and the browns, because to do anything else would have denied everything I had lived and believed for ten precious years of my life. Had I stayed, I would have denied myself, my hopes and dreams and my God. And then I would have been no man anymore.

I walked out and most of the congregation walked out with me. Some kept walking, and that hurts. Some people I have not seen since that day, and I know how deep the bitterness and hurt are for them, and in some cases for me. Betrayal either way is painful and it rends the universe in which I live.

Days later David told me that he had never expected anyone to join them outside. And when we all appeared, the caucus did not know what to do. They were unprepared— unprepared by years of betrayal, years of lies and false love. Maybe we were all unprepared.

I led the whites back into the parish hall, those who had walked out but were willing to see the crisis through, those who stayed in the church and could not understand what had happened, and we sat down to talk. We tried to understand what had happened and it took us several hours to do so. But we decided we had to accept the demands. We had to in order to live with ourselves and in order to preserve our Christian community. Bob Amussen, then a vestryman, now the senior warden (and an old friend), told me later that we must never forget we had acted to hold together a community of faith and love. Never lose that. Never lose the only act that ever really mattered.

I called an open vestry meeting for Thursday night and I hoped that everyone would come, that we could act as a body and within the law. Because whatever we did had to be done legally and securely. If we were to build again a church that had any meaning, what we decided had to be right and it had to stick.

The night of the meeting the parish hall was full. Everyone was there, and the vestry heard the people. Overwhelmingly we told the vestry to appoint four members of the caucus. We did so knowing that there were already three black men on our eleven-man vestry, and that four more would make a majority. We believed that was just. And we knew the people the caucus wanted on the vestry. Bert Gibson, the husband of our former parish secretary, a bright young accountant who had spent five years in the parish, who had spent many evenings in my home, whom I loved. Edyth Rogers, housewife and mother, active in Headstart, a member of the parish for ten years. I had buried her baby, her baby who had died in a rat-infested horror of a tenement. Since then, she had developed into a full, rich woman, seared by her sorrows, but strengthened, too. Eloise Booth, a member for fifteen years, who was working in a day-care center, divorced from her husband, and who had raised two lovely daughters with no man in the house. Those girls were my girls, too, and I loved them. And I loved Eloise. Maria Nieves, working in the Spanish community, a member of the parish for years. I had prepared her for confirmation. I had tried to help her raise her son in the terrors of our community, and we rejoiced that he seemed to be making it. That evening four whites resigned. Two in anger. Two to make the future.

Our junior warden, a lovely man who had just retired from

the advertising world and was abroad, wrote me saying that he did not really understand what the caucus was asking. He knew he could not understand, because he was not black. But if black people he loved said something was wrong, then he had to believe them. And that is how most of us felt.

When we discussed the money, a priest in our congregation, a sturdy man, respected by everyone there, told us the truth. He told us that for years we whites had gone into the black community to save it with dollars. We had told the blacks, Trust us, trust us to spend the money wisely in your behalf. Now the blacks wanted us to trust them. And we knew that was the issue. Our faith was on the line. We had to trust, or stop being Christians. We granted the money—and the reconciliation began.

I do not know what the future holds in store for us, for our people, for the nation. If we can make justice and love work out at St. Mark's, then maybe there is hope for all of us. If we cannot, I tremble for my people, I tremble for myself. Because none of us has been very good at hearing the truth. We have spoken about it so long and done it so little that we are unaccustomed. The church has been the great accommodation, the means whereby our society has lived with itself and perpetuated its lies. Peter Berger, the Christian sociologist, says our purpose and function has been to bless the OK society, to send people out of church unchanged, yet reinforced in their convictions that all is for the best in the best of all possible worlds.

But the ghetto cries out for freedom, cries out for justice, and tells us we are all wrong, that something has to change. And could that be the voice the Lord has chosen for this time and this place? The Lord who walked among the suffering and the hurt, who wept over Jerusalem, who led men out of captivity, may choose again to be among his wounded people.

And we know who the wounded are in our midst. Listen to them. Listen for the truth.

The image of different voices, different calls, different demands, is pretty basic to Christian theology. It is the basic image of Karl Barth's first book—*The Word of God and the Word of Man.* Man speaks and his voices resonate through the world. We hear him and we obey. But God's voice is to be heard in the land as well. Sometimes very softly, sometimes very loudly, but evoking creation, evoking justice and meaning and purpose, offering love to those who will accept it and act upon it. And will we obey him?

Each of us will have to make hard choices. The choice between truth and falsehood, the choice between life and death. We will hear many voices and many demands. Some will be lies. Some will be the truth, and the voice you obey will determine who you are. The voice this nation obeys will determine whether we grow in freedom or sink into terror and despotism. I know the voice of untruth. I can recognize Spiro Agnew. I have not forgotten Joe McCarthy's friend Richard Nixon, who plays to our worst fears and deepest darknesses. But it is hard to hear the truth. Desperately hard.

I cannot erase from my mind that moment at the altar of St. Mark's when I had to decide which voice to hear, which family to choose, which way to go. The whites in that congregation are in the world's eyes my brothers and sisters. They demand my loyalty. But in the family of Christ, those blacks and browns are my brothers and sisters. And my allegiance is to them. Jesus said we would have to choose. He said we would have to leave behind mothers and fathers, husbands and wives and follow him. And I think he meant we would have to choose new families, families that reflect the new world, that do not imprison us in the old. And the new family he had in mind was his family—potentially all of mankind, really far smaller, far weaker, hard to find, hard to live with, but life itself.

One of the reasons I love Martin Luther is for his stark and earthy images. He said once that man is an *ass*. Man is an ass always ridden by Christ or the devil. And if we are ridden by the devil, then we shall go to hell—and we shall never waver. And if we are ridden by Christ, then we are on the way to the kingdom of heaven. St. Augustine and John Calvin used the same image. But they said man was a horse. The truth was too painful for them—but not for Luther, who knew what dumb, pitiful creatures we really are surrounded by demons and temptations too strong to bear, always falling into the pit, always sinning. And that is why he told men to sin boldly. Because it is impossible not to sin. And the greatest of all sins is to believe you can avoid sin. No priest who ever heard a confession could ever believe in the innate righteousness of man. Not when he has heard the righteous and the moralistic, the judges and the critics, confess their sins. And how often they are in the very area they condemn so fiercely in others.

It is sinful to believe that you will not sin. It is sinful to believe you will ever be clean and just. A man is only just, he is only sinless if his standards are low enough. If my God demands very little of me, then perhaps I can obey, perhaps I can be good, as good men in my society are good. A small God produces small, proud men darkened in their imaginations, cruel to their fellowmen. But if a man worships the Lord of Lords, the God of Gods, then he knows that he lives in a sinful world in which men have corrupted the gift of life. And then such men have visions, visions of all the possibilities of life. They dream of freedom and of justice, they dream of worlds in which children will never starve, knowing the truth of this world. Perhaps it is the strength of the vision that allows them to be honest about their lives. So I think Martin Luther was speaking with some deep and inner joy when he spoke of the total depravity of man. Because all the beauty of the world, and there is much to be seen, all the grandeur of man, and there is much, is nothing but depravity before the splendor of God and the possibilities for human society and human life.

If a man has no hopes, then where is he, and how can he recognize the truth? And the truth of our world is best reflected in the face of God, in the vision of his glory.

The alternative is to find that cork-lined room where Marcel Proust hid, sanitary, airtight, unspotted with sin, and there alone and afraid die, slowly, terribly, knowing you have never lived.

Life means to me dancing to many tunes. Sometimes they are sad and sometimes they are happy, sometimes they are played by one musician and sometimes by another. But among all the tunes, above them, beneath them, is one great tune, varying in strength, varying in content, calling me in many ways, played by the Lord of creation. Or to use the image with which I began this book, a great song sung by a lion pacing back and forth across the land, singing his song and evoking creation and asking each of us to be part of his world. The only book I ever sat up all night to read was Havelock Ellis' *The Dance of Life*. And in the morning I wanted to dance. I wanted to leap up into the air and throw my legs out wide and my arms up and shout with joy.

The movie *Zorba the Greek* ends with Zorba and his boss, an uptight, sad little Englishman, dancing amidst the ruins of their hopes. Zorba had a wild dream of building a great chute down a mountainside to the beach. And up there on the mountain they could cut trees and shoot them down the side of the mountain to the sea. He and all the townspeople had spent months building the great machine, months of sweat and devotion. And then the great day came, and the first log careened down the mountainside—and it carried the chute with it. The whole device collapsed, and everything was lost. Zorba and his master stood alone, humiliated, hurt, destroyed. And what else is there to do but dance? And dance they do, to a wild Greek tune, on the beach, alone, madly, gaily, joyfully dancing. So the movie ends. But the Englishman is now alive. He is a man. And there is no limit to what a man can do.

My great disappointment is that I cannot dance. And I know somehow that the day I can, the day I can really dance and with my body express all my sorrows and all my joys, then I will be a man. And now, I am just another creature on the way, on the way to being a man.

The greatest pastoral mistake I ever made, in any case the one that shames me the most, was with a lovely woman, one of those women whom I hold infinitely dear to me. Her husband had died after years of illness and she was absolutely broken. I could see her drained face, her empty eyes, her broken heart. She could not face life. She could not face death. And in the midst of her grief I said to her, "Yet a little while," and then you will be alive. The world will once again be joyful and real. You will not be dead forever. But I had blasphemed, I had denied life. I had denied that this terrible moment, this moment of hideous grief was life. It is life, as fully life as the moments of joy. And the man who cannot live the one cannot live the other. No man can select the kind of life he wants, the moments he chooses and the moments he rejects. A man lives always or he lives never.

One of the great Biblical images is that of the mustard seed. Jesus holds up a mustard seed and says, This is a mustard tree. It is big enough to give shade, big enough for birds to build their nests in. Of course this is absurd. It is only a mustard seed. But it is the truth nonetheless. Because a mustard seed will be—is—a mustard tree or it is nothing at all. There are no other options. Just as an orange seed is an orange tree or nothing at all. And men are men or they are nothing. In God's providence we have been called to rich and varied, sad and lonely lives. We have no choice. We become what we are or nothing at all.

It was only months after I saw *Zorba the Greek* that I suddenly understood what it was all about. There on the beach in the midst of their failure, of their death, they dance. Zorba dances and rejoices. And then I knew that this glorious tale is about the Christ—the resurrected Christ. Man as the Lord proclaims him to be. So I read the book and in it I found the New Testament everywhere, the testament of hope and life.

Zorba is talking to his boss about what it means to make a pot on a wheel, of the wild joy and the incredible demand of creation. And in the telling he explains that he cut off his finger in order better to make the pot.

" 'Well,' I asked, 'what about your finger?'

" 'Oh, it got in my way in the wheel. It always got plumb in the middle of things and upset my plan so one day I used a hatchet.'

" 'Didn't it hurt you?'

" 'What do you mean? I'm not a tree trunk—of course it hurt me, but it got in my way at the wheel. So I cut it off.' "

"I felt as I listened to Zorba that the world was recovering its pristine freshness. All the dulled daily things regained the brightness they had in the beginning, when we came out of the hands of God. Water, women, the stars, bread, returned to their mysterious, primitive origin and the divine whirlwind burst once more upon the air."

Kazantzakis knows his New Testament well and knows that nothing must stand in the way of life, of creation.

Sometimes I think that perhaps I have grown up after all. I have begun to relax about all the dangers, to know that I cannot grasp at life because it always gets out of my hands. I cannot clutch at love. So I begin to let myself go and I accept defeat, the letting go of all the things I clung to. And then I begin to win. It is strange, though. It is a little like the Zen story of the man who is hanging by his fingertips from a precipice, thousands of feet above the rapids; he has been hanging there for hours. What will he do? Let go, of course. What else can he do? What else can a man do who knows his life is in God's hands to be played out to its full meaning? But it will never have meaning if I cannot let go, if I cannot listen for the music, for the demands, for those radical moments in which the Lord re-creates me and moves me toward my manhood.

But this does not mean playing games or presuming on God. It means making moral decisions. As Zorba does, who is alive and free. Free to make the wrong decisions and repent, free enough to make the right decisions and rejoice. The Englishman cannot make decisions. He is not alive. He cannot act, and until the moment when there is nothing left for him to cling to, until all his money and all his hope are gone and he is drowning, he cannot dance. And the man who cannot dance is not alive. I suspect this is why Jesus told the dead to go bury their dead. If you are not ready to live right now, then there is really nothing for you to do but to join the dead. Let the dead bury the dead, and let the living join me.

My own favorite Biblical character is David. In seminary I studied Hebrew with Dean Taylor. I would have studied anything he taught. But I am certainly glad it was Hebrew and not basket weaving. And for him I had to translate the story of David and Bathsheba. And as I read it, I saw how hearty and lusty a story it was, and how pallid we tried to make it with our moralistic translations. To be fully understood, the story needs a fair sprinkling of the kind of short, crisp Anglo-Saxon words the dead hate to hear.

It is one of the funniest stories ever written. It starts with the line, "When the time of year came for kings to go forth to battle, David sent Joab." David sent a soldier and he stayed home. And even kings, when time hangs heavy on their hands, can go very wrong. He saw Bathsheba sunning herself on the roof—and he took her. And they had a grand time, except that he got her pregnant. And even kings have to be careful about impregnating the wives of their courtiers. So he brought her husband back from the front to get himself off the hook. But Uriah was the greatest boy scout in history, and he would not go home to his wife. He told the king that if his men had to sleep in tents and alone, so would he. David got him drunk. The dancing girls tried to stimulate him. But he would not go home. So David killed him, and in an awful sense he almost deserved to die for being such a fool. But a king before God is just another man, and there is a price for murder. There is a price for adultery. For David it was the death of his child by Bathsheba. So the story switches the image from the proud and cruel and lustful man, to the sorrowful and hurt man, the man who watches his child die and who ponders his own crime.

When his son dies, David gets up from his knees, washes himself, and orders dinner. When the servants come, they are shocked and question him. You wept and prayed while the child was alive, and now that he is dead, you do this. And David answers, "While the boy was still alive I fasted and wept, thinking, 'It may be that the Lord will be gracious to me, and the boy may live.' But now that he is dead, why should I fast? Can I bring him back again? I shall go to him; he will not come back to me."

David scaled the heights and plumbed the depths. He risked everything. He lost everything. He gained everything. The crimes he committed, the anguish afterwards were also the avenues of God's grace, to the building of the man into a giant figure. And somehow this story proclaims the necessity of living boldly, sinning boldly, because there is no other road to manhood except the road of life.

In my own life the test came with the sickness of my little boy. He was ten years old, and we discovered that he had a brain tumor, a ghastly tumor on the pituitary gland, right in the middle of the head. "A benign tumor," the doctor said, "in the most malign area of the brain." My wife and I never thought he would live, and we found ourselves coming apart as people. A beautiful man, Daniel Corrigan, a bishop of our church, came to see us, and he told us of the death of his son in World War II. And he told us how it felt, and how he managed to live through it. And that was the greatest pastoral ministry anyone had ever given us—the ministry of truth and of experience. Because I am sure that when a man shares his experience with another, he ennobles them both. He says that my experience is precious to me. It makes me a man. So yours is precious, too, and makes you a man.

Tommy was going to be operated on Easter Tuesday, and neither of us believed he would live. All of Holy Week I prayed that the Lord would spare my child. "Don't take my little boy away from me," I pleaded with my God. And slowly that other truth, that honesty which comes up from inside and which must be the voice of the Lord, said to me, But he is not your child. He is not your possession. He did not come into this world for your happiness or pleasure. He did not come to be a comfort in your old age. He is God's child, and he came into this world to work out his own destiny. Pray for him, that the Lord will make something out of this for him.

Good Friday I preached on the story of Abraham and Isaac, and I tried to tell the people what was happening to me and what I believe. I do not know what anyone heard. I only know what I said to myself. And I knew that it did not matter why Abraham had to sacrifice his son. That is not the point of the story. Any more than it mattered to me why Tommy was sick. All that mattered was how to live in the midst of this sorrow, how to give up my son, and then, when he survived surgery, how to take him back and start a new life together.

Somewhere in the midst of that experience, Bishop Corrigan told me to remember that my sorrow would make me a man. I would never again be the same, never free to take life lightly, never free to be cold and unmoved. Now I would experience compassion and sorrow as I had never known them before, and always thereafter be a richer and fuller man. I hope Tommy somehow will be able to make something out of this terrible experience and grow up to be a fuller and richer man himself. That I can hope for. We have suffered too much together for either of our lives to be wasted.

It seems to me that life is full of risks that we can face because we know we have been forgiven, because, as Karl Barth says, men are always wrong before God. And therefore we are free. We are free to make our mistakes, and grow, and live. If I thought I lived in a world where someone was keeping score, I do not know if I could go on. I do not know what I would do. But we can take the risks, because we can afford to, because we know that we are God's troubled and troublesome people wandering in the desert, grumbling, murmuring, complaining all the time. But our Puritan fathers knew that we were there for a purpose—and the purpose was to reach the Promised Land, to go there led by our Lord, fed by his body and blood, and eager to make the journey.

Moby Dick, I think, is the nineteenth-century American Book of Job, and therefore it is about how men survive in a world which they cannot understand and barely can deal with. There is a little chapter tucked away in that great book about Bulkington, who speaks to his friends in the sailors' bar and tells them about the men who go to sea. They are no different from the men who stay at home in their warm houses. Some are good, some are bad. Some face their problems and some do not. And the only difference is that some have gone to sea. And a man who has never been to sea will never know what that means. He will never know what it means to challenge the sea, to change the whole way of life from acceptance of the land to the challenging of the sea. The book itself is about a crazy captain and a crazy crew who go to sea to challenge the white whale. Ahab has lost his leg to that whale, and only the whale can give him his answer. So he must encounter that whale. He must find him in order to find himself, to find his leg, to be whole. And he does find the whale, and in the encounter the whale destroys him. But who says this is not the victory of man who in encountering life is consumed by it—but has lived it in the process? It is a very enigmatic kind of book, but then I think life is very enigmatic and most of its riddles will never be discovered. Just as Martin Buber says of God—"God cannot be described. He can only be encountered." So it is with life.

My son asked me the other day in a moment of anger and confusion what it was I really stood for, what it was I was doing, what did I think it was all about? And the only answer I could give him was that somehow I have lived as fully as I know how. I have tried to respond to the moment as best I could, and I have tried to be free. I know I have had no consistent goal. So when a friend remarked that I had no consistency in me, first I was terribly hurt, and then I realized he had told me the truth that I hoped would be true, that my consistency can only come in obedience, that the consistency can never be in my life, but in the Lord of my life. I wanted to tell my son that the only hope I have is to go on living as fully as possible so that when the day comes that I die, whether it is now or later, I will be ready to go, because I will know that I have lived my life and not wasted it or lost it. I do not want it to be sand running through my fingers, or anybody else's fingers, but a life that finally has a goal.

There is a book of the Bible which really is an old man's book, Ecclesiastes. When I was in seminary I hated it, and I am glad I did, because I was not ready for it. But now I can begin to see it and understand it. It was written by an old and wise man, a man who lived life very fully and very richly. No man was ever so ribald and full of life as this one. And when he speaks of all his concubines as man's delight, then I know he lived. He tells of all his life and all his experiences, and he has experienced everything and known everything there is for man to know. He has tasted life's treachery and depravity. He has tasted its grandeur and nobility, and he has searched out all its meaning. From this pinnacle and only from this pinnacle he knows that everything is vanity except to live in the hand of God. And that is life. But none of us can come to that understanding too soon. Only an old and wise man can really understand it. But do not come in by the back door. I think of all those little old men of twenty who already know the vanity of life without ever having lived it and therefore are sad beyond belief.

Life is a long, hard road, and at the end is the heavenly city. The greatest book in the English language I think is *Pilgrim's*

Progress. My grandmother had two books on her living room table—the Bible and *Pilgrim's Progress*—as every Puritan home had. And as she could not tell the difference between her childhood and the Bible, neither could she tell the difference between *Pilgrim's Progress* and the Bible, because they are interchangeable. Pilgrim walks down a long and lonely road beset with all sorts of terrors and anxieties and comes finally to the heavenly city. And along the way the Lord sends man after man to help him down the road, to give substance to his life. And from time to time he gives us glimpses of the Promised Land, the glimpses that keep us on the road. I think they saw some glimpses out in Ocean Hill. I think we saw some last winter at St. Mark's. I think we will see some more and we will be richer for it. But there will be a lot of hard moments ahead and there will be many dangers on the road. And the only thing I know a man can do as he walks down the road is not to walk at all, but to dance because he believes that a great lion is singing a song calling him to dance, to create, to join in the lion's task of building a glorious new world. I want to dance with that lion.

11

A few months after the confrontation, Nell and Bert Gibson asked me to baptize their little boy, Bertram Maxwell Gibson III, "Third" for short. And I did. The service that Sunday began with black poems read by black people. We sang great black music and I preached for Nell, for Bert, for Third, and for me. This is how the sermon went:

There hasn't been any preaching in this church for quite a while. The reason there hasn't been any is because, when the preacher stands up, he's got to preach from the soul of the people, from his own soul. No man preaches from a broken soul. No man can preach from a broken people. It's only as we come together that maybe that can happen. Nell, who is one of those women I love very deeply, asked me to preach, so I'm going to try. You're going to have to help me. This is the way I'm going to begin.

Little black baby, we're going to baptize you now. We're going to bury you in your grave like the people Israel were buried in the water. Like the Lord Jesus went to the cross and died. We're taking you to your grave now. We're not going to wait till later. We're not going to let you die at the hands of a society that doesn't know how to live. We're going to let you die now so you can begin to live. Then we're going to watch you rise up out of this grave that we're going to dig for you today and out of this water, rise up to be a man and to walk with your head up, your shoulders back and to walk with a light in your eyes. You're going to lead your people to the Promised Land. You're going to lead them because you're going to follow the Lord, because that's the promise we're making for you today.

I had trouble even writing that, because that's a fantastic thing to say to a child or to say to ourselves or to believe, but if I didn't say that, what would I say? Am I going to tell him that he hasn't got any hope? That this is a society that consigns black babies to nothing? And doesn't know that it consigns white babies to nothing, too? Should I stand up here and tell him he's going to go to a rotten school and be crippled before he even begins to live and that's true for white children just as much as for black? That he's never going to work at a job that's equal to his potential? Am I going to say that? Tell him that he's going to live like a slave for the rest of his life? Shall I tell a white baby that he, too, is going to live like a slave, all the rest of his life a slave to pettiness and to tiny gods and to a flag we don't understand, cheap politicians, the slavery of being oppressed and being the oppressor? Shall I tell him that he's going to grow up to be smaller than he was created to be, and then live in guilt because he knows he's smaller than he was created to be? Can't get out of that awful bind of being a little creature in God's big world? If I told him that, then he never would grow up to be a man. Our society tells child after child after child this. Not necessarily in words, but in what we do. No wonder they don't grow up.

Or are you prepared—are we all prepared—to tell him the greater truth, the far greater truth, that a child can die to this, can die to this world; he can die to its petty gods and its brassy idols? He can die to trivia and foolishness and he can walk in the shining light. Are you prepared to tell this little child, this little impressionable child, that he can live in dignity and in beauty and that he can help create a whole new world and a new people and new hope? And if you're prepared to tell him that, you can only do so if you believe it yourself. You can't mouth little niceties about God and hope and all these things if they mean nothing to you. The polls tell us eighty-five percent of the American people believe in God. But they don't know his name, don't know his love, don't know his judgment. If you're a slave, your child's going to be a slave, because he'll know nothing else. Unless you're ready to believe, there's nothing you're going to tell that child.

But it's hard to believe. And there's so much around you that says, Don't, don't believe, don't hope, don't live—take the money and run, which might as well be the epitaph of our society. And yet, if you've been trained, if you've tried over the years to listen to the deeper sound, to go down deeper into your fellowmen and deeper into yourself, maybe you've heard other sounds. Maybe you've seen other sights. You could teach him, if you believed it yourself, that at the center of this universe there is justice, there is love, there is dignity. That this is what men were created to live with, by and for. If you believe it yourself, you can teach him that the God of history wars against his people all the time. Every minute of the day and night he wars against us, trying to make us free, trying to make a new world, even though we don't want to let go of the old one. We don't want to let go of the tiny gods, because tiny as they are, they're better than the unknown that we won't believe. But if you can listen to that, if you can listen to the greater hopes, and if you can teach him in the way you act and the way you feel and the way you dance and the way you cry that there's something more in this world and there's something deeper, then he's going to grow up to be a man.

I'd like to tell you to bring him into the church every day from now on out. But I can't tell you that, because the church isn't what it was meant to be, and it isn't what it says it is. But somewhere, sometimes in the church and sometimes somewhere else, there's a family of people who live by God's grace and who live in justice, who live in the Promised Land. Maybe nobody else sees it, but they see it in their hearts and they live that way. And these people live as if the world were a just world. Live as if they were free. Live as if everything new had already come. Somewhere in every town there's a family like that and it's going to be up to you to find that family, for this little black baby. So that he'll grow up trained in the very depth of his being to hear other voices and to see other sights.

See, if he dies now, and if you die now, there's nothing ever to be afraid of again. You don't have to worry about any death that society can inflict on you, because you're dead already, man. There's nothing that anybody can do. And then you can start living and live without chains and live in hope. That's the gift that you and I are promising to offer this little boy. Be sure you know what the gift is. Be sure you're willing to take him to the cross. And believe that you'll find there resurrection and hope and beauty.